BALI'S SON

Uncovering Life's Hidden Blessings

Luca De Coney

Dedication

For my son,

You are the living reflection of every lesson, every blessing, and every truth I spent a lifetime seeking across two worlds. Your existence gave my story meaning and inspired me to understand my own.

For my family,

To the family and friends who grounded me in Bali and lifted me in the West — your love carried me further than any place ever could. To Made and Brate, who raised me with a love deeper than circumstance and showed me that home is a bond of spirit, not blood. And to my parents, Marta and John, whose brief presence shaped the beginning of my journey and whose memory continues to walk beside me. Your love, in all its forms, lives within these pages.

For the friends who shaped my path,

Whether your name appears in these chapters or not, know that your presence has never been forgotten. Your influence lives quietly within me, shaped into the moments, lessons, and memories that built this story.

For my partner,

Who offered the quiet guidance, patience, and love that helped carry this story from my heart onto the page. With deepest love and gratitude.

Table of Contents

About this Book

What is the hidden cost of paradise?

This is the question at the heart of *Bali's Son: Uncovering Life's Hidden Blessings* — a memoir that trades the tropical cliché of palm trees and tranquility for the profound, often challenging reality of a life lived at the ultimate cultural crossroads.

Born to a charismatic Australian-American design mogul and a vibrant Italian artist, my early years unfolded in a world of bamboo mansions, celebrity clients, and relentless artistic ambition. However, this golden existence was built on fault lines: the tragic loss of my mother at a young age, the emotional vacuum left by her absence, and a complex, improvised family structure woven together by my Balinese "mom" Berate. This book takes you into the heart of that paradox, exploring what happens when the relentless pursuit of Western dreams collides with the spiritual, ancient soul of Bali.

This is more than a story of exotic locales; it is a search for belonging. It chronicles my journey to reconcile a life defined by stark opposites: the discipline of a traditional Balinese upbringing versus the free-spirited chaos of my Western heritage; the simple comforts of a communal village against the sophistication of an international jet-set life. From the daily rituals of Canang Sari offerings on the temple grounds to the dizzying reality of attending international schools, the narrative lays bare the fundamental identity struggle of a boy caught between two incompatible worlds.

At its core, *Bali's Son* is about transforming inherited pain into profound purpose. It is a raw, introspective look at the complexities of love, the destructive force of unaddressed mental health struggles, and the enduring resilience required to heal from early trauma. As a whole, the book argues that the greatest blessings in life are often disguised as our hardest challenges — that within every loss, there is a lesson waiting to be uncovered, and within every struggle for identity, a clearer sense of self waiting to emerge.

For anyone who has ever wrestled with the question "Where do I truly belong?" or sought to understand the lasting influence of the family we inherit, this memoir serves as a mirror. It is an invitation to look beyond the surface of life's trials and discover the essential, hidden truths that shape the human spirit.

Introduction

Every story begins somewhere, but not every beginning is clear. Mine starts on the island of Bali, an island draped in mysticism, culture, and unparalleled beauty. It is a place where the scent of incense mingles with ocean breezes, where spirituality hums in the air, and where life flows to the rhythm of offerings and rituals. This island wasn't just my home; it was my cradle, my teacher, and the foundation upon which my identity was built. But as with any great story, the foundation was just the beginning.

I was born into a world of fundamental contrasts. On one side, I inherited a lineage steeped in Balinese tradition, with its reverence for spirits, the strength of community, and the essential pursuit of cosmic balance. On the other, I was tethered to a powerful Western influence that brought opportunity, complexity, and at times, an alien sense of individuality.

Navigating these two worlds was a challenge, and the crucible that forged my character. I had to reconcile the simplicity of a culture rooted in harmony with the often chaotic pull of ambition and modernity. It wasn't always easy, and there were moments when the two worlds clashed, leaving me unsure of where I belonged.

This memoir is not a story of easy successes or smooth journeys. It is a raw tapestry woven with struggles, triumphs, heartbreak, and profound growth. It is a reflection on life's fundamental unpredictability, where moments of clarity and purpose often arrive wrapped in confusion and pain.

From losing loved ones to finding a renewed sense of purpose, from the confines of a strict but loving upbringing to the unshackled adventures of adulthood, this is a story of becoming. Becoming a son, a partner, a father, and most importantly, myself.

Throughout these pages, you will find the lessons that life has imparted to me — not in neat, easily digestible packages, but through experiences that tested my resolve, my values, and my very sense of self and place in this world. You will see a boy who yearned for freedom yet struggled to understand its weight, and a young man who stumbled, failed, and often fought against his own limitations, only to realize that every stumble was, in fact, a crucial step forward.

You will meet the people who shaped me, for better or worse. This is not just my personal story; it is a story about family — the one you are born into and the one you create. It is a story about identity, how it forms and reforms in the face of life's trials. And it is a story about balance, about finding harmony in a world that often feels at odds with itself.

The chapters ahead are a journey through time, space, and emotion. From the shores of Bali to the bustling streets of Australia, from the serenity of meditation to the chaos of family dynamics, I have strived to lay it all bare. My hope is that as you read, you will find glimpses of your own journey in mine — moments of struggle, clarity, and growth that resonate with your own experiences.

Let this book be more than a recounting of my life. Let it be an invitation to reflect on your own. Just as Bali taught me the value of balance and harmony and the world taught me the power of perspective, perhaps my story can offer you a new way of seeing the hidden blessings within your own life.

Prologue

Back to the Roots

As we embark on life's journey, the allure of our origins often intensifies, whispering to us through the winds of change and the shifting sands of time. In the following pages, we will trace the path back to the roots, to the very soil that once nurtured the earliest blossoms of our identity and purpose. Here, nestled within the sacred contours of Bali, we will rediscover the fundamental truths that shape our being. Though you are accompanying me on my journey, my wish is that you will apply my experiences and epiphanies to your own.

"Back to the Roots" is not merely a return to a geographical location; it is an exploration of the soul's landscape, a deep dive into the waters of self that reveal the reflections of who we were, who we are, and who we might become. This journey is about grounding ourselves in the familiar yet often forgotten terrains of our past, gathering the wisdom scattered along the paths we once walked.

As you traverse these pages, let the stories serve as both mirrors and windows — mirrors that reflect your own experiences of returning to your beginnings and windows that open to new vistas of understanding. Each narrative woven into this chapter carries the subtle scent of introspection and the vibrant colors of transformation.

This return is a pilgrimage of the spirit, an odyssey that challenges us to reconcile the past with the present, to integrate the lessons learned with the life we currently live. It is an invitation to pause, breathe, and reflect on the essence of coming home — to a place, to a people, and most profoundly, to oneself.

Let the journey begin.

Cast of Characters

- **Luca:** The author and narrator; son of Marta and John.

- **Marta**: My birth mother. The woman who gave me life.

- **John**: My birth father and the architect of our complex family.

My Western Family

- **Marion (Marie):** My stepmother. A maternal figure who raised my eldest sisters.

- **Wayan:** My oldest sister.

- **Made:** My second sister. She served as my custodian and maternal anchor, raising me with a mother's care after I lost my own.

- **Donaldine (Didi):** My stepmother, Ziska's mother.

- **Ziska:** My third sister; a protective presence in my early years.

- **Silvia:** My stepmother.

- **Lily:** Made's daughter and my niece.

My Balinese Family

- **Nyoman Berate:** My Balinese mother. The woman who opened her heart and home to me in Bali.

- **Nyoman Dayuh (Unyil):** My Balinese father. A man of tradition and the pillar of my life in the village.

- **Made:** Berate and Nyoman's first son. My Balinese brother and constant companion.

- **Komang:** Berate and Nyoman's second son. My youngest Balinese brother.

CHAPTER I

Turning Challenges into Stepping Stones

> *We are not one story, but many stories woven together.*

John, My Father

The ocean-laced air of Manly, Sydney, Australia, provided John De Coney's first breath. His early life was not carved by the predictable path of school bells and classrooms. At the raw age of eight, a decisive choice was made — not out of idle rebellion, but from a profound necessity and a spirit already alight with entrepreneurship. While his mother, Jean, dedicated her tireless hours to the Australian embassy, young John claimed the bustling, sun-drenched streets as his true school. He became a blur of motion on his bicycle, a permanent fixture pedaling around town, selling newspapers. By the time he was ten, he carried the weighty resilience of a man twice his age, a Marlboro often hanging loosely from his lips as he hawked the morning news. For John, challenges weren't roadblocks; they were rough-hewn stepping stones to a greater height. His ferocious work ethic was less about a paycheck and more about an unquenchable thirst to learn and master whatever life tossed his way.

At seventeen, the rhythm of his life shifted seismically. John and Jean traded the familiar sands of Sydney for the relentless, electric pulse of New York City. It was a landscape of dreams, and Jean, ever the opportunist, steered her son toward the infinite possibilities of the hairdressing world.

John didn't test the waters; he dove into the deep end. Securing a position as a hairdressing assistant to the renowned Paul McGregor was merely the first strike of the match. His days were spent learning the contours of style, his evenings navigating a chaotic, beautiful life as a nanny to Paul's five children. What might have crushed another was simply another skill to be conquered, another adventure to be cataloged.

His ambition, a burning torch, next led him to the hallowed halls of the Vidal Sassoon shop, a gold-plated apprenticeship. Here, he didn't just hone his craft; he built a brotherhood. Shared dreams and aspirations with Vinny Pascal, Simon Scudero, and Paul Ropp cemented them as lifelong friends. John's star was ascending rapidly; he styled numerous celebrities and forged a powerful, visionary friendship with Paul Mitchell, then an assistant at the Aston salon.

The culmination of this growth arrived when John turned twenty-three. With the unwavering endorsement of actress Cybil Shepherd, he opened his own salon at 882 Madison Avenue. The space instantly became the throbbing heart of Hollywood's early 70s hair epicenter; a magnet for the era's brightest stars: Liza Minnelli, the Rolling Stones, Rod McDonald, Peter Allan, and Jordan Christopher.

But the heart, as always, had its own capricious journey. A momentary escape from his empire took John to Brazil. In the humid, frenetic chaos of Rio de Janeiro, he met Marion at a friend's house. He was immediately smitten, but thwarted by the presence of a boyfriend at her side. Fate, however, rarely accepts a first refusal. A week later, their paths converged again on a private cruise boat gliding through the serene waters off Angra dos Reis, and a love affair, unpredictable and profound, began to bloom amidst Brazil's beauty.

Back amongst the relentless energy of New York, John, now a notable figure in the city's style vanguard, engineered the next chapter. He invited Marion to trade her Brazilian home for the sleepless, towering metropolis. She accepted, leading to an instant marriage, captivated by his charisma and their coalescing dreams. Their love deepened against the backdrop of skyscrapers, and John knew this was no fleeting passion; she was the one. The proposal, as bold as his personality, unfolded in the city's iconic green sanctuary, Central Park. On a crisp, clear day, surrounded by a trusted circle of friends who had become family, he dropped to one knee. The park's lush scenery bore silent witness to the magical moment.

Their joy, however, was immediately met with the cold stone of bureaucracy. When the universal church priest attempted to register the marriage at City Hall, the papers were refused. The reason? Central Park was not a legally recognized venue for marriage. Unwilling to let arbitrary rules diminish their love, John made a dramatic move, leveraging his fame to spotlight their cause and advocate for marriage rights in the park. He took the civil rights battle to court. The legal skirmish that followed became an epic stand for love against rigid regulation. John argued that affection should not be caged by boundary lines, insisting that a public space, cherished by the multitudes, should be open to the celebration of profound human connection. The case became a media sensation, drawing public scrutiny.

The victory was not just John's; it was a triumph for romantics everywhere. In a landmark decision, Central Park became a legally recognized venue for marriage, a precedent sealed by the couple's stubborn love. The resulting fame was immediate, their love story plastered across headlines, pulling them into a vortex of media attention. John and Marion, now longing for a quiet, private existence, made a bold choice: they would leave the New York frenzy behind to embark on a journey around the world. John placed his successful salon into the capable hands of his trusted colleagues, certain of his legacy.

Their global travels led them to Japan, a country that offered John a unique interlude from 1973 to 1974. There, he spent a year fully immersed in teaching hairdressing, a testament to his adaptability and the indelible mark he left on the craft across continents.

Their adventure continued as they sailed through Asian waters, fueled by a shared spirit of liberty that Marion often encapsulated with one word: they were "freaks". In 1974, they landed in Bali, the island of mysticism, to forge a new life far removed from conventionality. The island's rustic charm was immediately apparent; on their first day, the quaint bamboo hut that served as their bungalow was finally wired for electricity, a sign of Bali's slow, deliberate development. Bali became a blank canvas for their free-spirited creativity.

Their attention was quickly captured by the island's deep-rooted tradition of bamboo craftsmanship. Driven by this intrigue, they ventured inland to the village of Tying Tutul, or "spotted wood," hunting for the hands of a master artisan. Initial attempts were frustrating, but serendipity intervened at a modest *warung* — a small shop selling snacks and drinks. There they found Pak Nyoman, a local man who embodied the warm hospitality of the Balinese people and, crucially, the person they needed to help recruit workers to bring their modern bamboo designs to life.

Their passion soon manifested in a physical structure: their own home, a unique and stunning blend of bamboo and ironwood. It was a personal sanctuary and a bold, three-dimensional testament to their innovative design. The house was impossible to ignore, soon drawing the gaze of the local expatriate community. John and Marion (now Marie) recognized a lucrative niche in customizing homes for these foreigners, specializing in integrating the traditional Balinese *bedeg* (patterned bamboo weaves, typically used for mats) into contemporary living spaces. John's growing expertise in this delicate art earned him a moniker that resonated across the island: "John Bedeg".

To scale the venture, John needed to formalize it. However, Indonesian law was a fortress; foreigners were barred from owning companies in their own names. The solution was a cultural bridge, a pragmatic and respectful alliance forged with Pak Nyoman. Together they founded Bali Bedeg, a company that was more than a business; it was a living tribute to traditional craftsmanship and eco-conscious design, transforming the architectural use of ironwood and bamboo and bridging the cultural gap between foreign vision and local skill.

In their new island life, John and Marie's family expanded. Their first daughter, Wayan, was born in Goa, India, in 1977. This unusual birthplace was a necessity, circumventing the Balinese regulations that prohibited foreigners on tourist visas from having children on the island. Two years later, in 1979, they welcomed their second daughter, Made, born in Bali. In keeping with the island's deep heritage, their children were named to signify their birth order, a reflection of the family's integration into the Balinese community. Their unique life was a magnet, drawing friends from around the globe, some of whom became so enchanted, they chose to plant their own roots in the tropical paradise.

However, even paradise has its shadows. Marie's adventurous spirit, though initially drawn to Bali, began to yearn for a different horizon, a new experience beyond the life they had painstakingly built. The longing led her to a difficult, definitive choice: she returned to Brazil, taking Wayan and Made with her. John, heartbroken but resolute, remained in Bali, his dedication to his craft and the community unshakeable.

It was at the custom bamboo home he and Marie had designed that John's life took its next extraordinary leap. His old friend, Paul Mitchell, came to visit. Paul saw the remarkable homes John had built, and over lunch at John's table, he offered an unimaginable opportunity - to design and construct his personal estate in Hawaii. The moment was electric. John seized an Indonesian hundred Rupiah-cent coin from the table, held it aloft, and declared, "Here, this is what I'm going to build for you." The coin featured the image of a traditional house, a *Rumah Gadang*, rooted in the Minangkabau culture of West Sumatra.

John's final design was a masterpiece of collaborative vision. He re-engineered the traditional form, infusing it with intricate Balinese carvings. The final structure was a majestic edifice built entirely from iron-wood, without a single nail or piece of metal, a profound tribute to sustainability and traditional Balinese craftsmanship. The construction was an epic undertaking: the entire mansion was built in Bali, then meticulously deconstructed, with every piece cataloged before being loaded into containers and shipped across the vast ocean to the Island of Maui, Hawaii.

The project grew grander still when Paul and John decided that only the original artisans could re-assemble the house. For the first time in Bali's history,

John chartered a flight for forty-two skilled Balinese craftsmen to Maui. Many had never left their homeland or seen the inside of an airplane, so for them, the journey was a transformative cultural earthquake. In Maui, they worked their magic, rebuilding the mansion with the same spirit and skill that had birthed it in Bali. The completion of the estate became the pinnacle of their lives, a symbol of their dedication. John and his team, including his foreman and partner, Pak Nyoman, reaped the rewards. The returning craftsmen used their earnings to establish their own businesses and afford luxuries that were previously unimaginable.

The echo of this massive, unconventional construction project resonated globally. John was recognized, even within Indonesian political circles, as the first person in Bali to create and export homes off the island, forging opportunities for local craftsmen beyond their shores. Buoyed by this success, Paul Mitchell proposed yet another ambitious project: seven themed homes in Hawaii, each with a unique concept. John embraced the challenge, developing innovative designs and bringing them to life in Bali.

However, a tragic shadow fell across the venture: Paul Mitchell passed away midway through the design phase. Though the homes were fully conceptualized in Bali, they were never realized on the Hawaiian shore. They were eventually dismantled and stored away for a future sale that never came.

John achieved this remarkable success without a single official certification — neither as a licensed architect nor a certified hairdresser. His triumphs were a pure function of his unconventional genius and collaborative spirit. Beyond his professional feats, John's charisma and generosity defined him. He welcomed locals into his home with open arms, cultivating a sense of community and warmth that harked back to an era of genuine island camaraderie.

His home in Legian, nestled in the charming stretch between the bustling towns of Seminyak and Kuta, was a perpetual crossroads. It was a vibrant haven of hospitality where diverse, intriguing individuals from around the world met and mingled. In this rich, human mosaic, a new connection was destined to be woven: he would meet Didi.

Didi

Donaldine, or Didi as she is known, carried the complexity of her heritage — British polish layered over colorful Sri Lankan roots. Her story began with a quiet sorrow: the passing of her mother. In the early 1950s, at the tender age of four, her father decided to emigrate to England. Almost immediately, the walls of a boarding school became her refuge and her classroom. She grew into a passionate woman, eventually becoming a primary school teacher. During this time, she became involved in starting up a drama workshop for the school, through which she choreographed the dance routines for the drama productions.

In the late 1970s she returned to Goldsmiths College for a BH degree to continue her studies in dance education. It was during this time that an unexpected ripple occurred. Attending a house party in London, Didi met Lawrence who was showing a movie he filmed about Indonesia. Subsequently he introduced her to Suzy who was bringing clothes, handicrafts back to England. In order to help fund her studies Didi started to sell leftover stock to friends privately.

Later the working relationship with Suzy deepened into friendship. Late 1978, Didi received an irresistible invitation: a trip to Bali to source goods firsthand. She accepted immediately, driven not just by a new business venture but by an urge to finally touch a part of the world she had only seen through a lens.

In Bali, the social fabric was tightly woven — the phrase "everybody knows everybody" was gospel. It was through this close-knit network that, in 1987, when Didi returned to Bali, she met John. Introduced by a mutual friend named Danyal, she visited John's home while he was mourning the loss of someone dear to him. What began as a quiet gesture of support quickly evolved into a deep, lasting bond. By the end of 1987, their friendship had ignited into a relationship. Their new life soon took them to Hawaii, where John was consumed by the ambitious construction of Paul Mitchell's private estate, and later, the planning for seven subsequent themed homes — a grand vision tragically cut short by Mitchell's passing.

The news of the pregnancy in 1988 prompted a moment of stark, quiet honesty between them. As Didi, facing her own medical complications decided to fly to Melbourne, Australia, for the birth — a practical necessity given her age and the need for medical certainty — the scaffolding of their romantic relationship began to creak. In the silence of her hospital room, far from the frenetic energy of Bali, they faced a difficult truth: the powerful connection they shared was less a burning fire and more the steady, reliable warmth of a shared history. A profound friendship, yes, but the wild, romantic destiny they'd chased felt untethered. Their paths, though still linked, had found different gravity.

After Ziska was born, she fully immersed herself into the all-consuming wonderful world of motherhood. She returned to Bali and decided to live in Legian close to John as she wanted Ziska to grow up knowing her father. Meanwhile, John was immediately pulled back to Bali, drawn by his enterprises, the constant rhythm of construction, and his thriving social life. He was completely involved by the complex machinery of his wooden houses for the Paul Mitchell project. He was a loving father, appearing for visits with grand gestures, strict in ways, often focused on instilling a firm moral compass while remaining distant from the daily, messy reality of raising a child. Their connection, having moved past romance, settled into a unique, functional orbit: a dedicated co-parenting anchored by an enduring and loving friendship.

Marta, My Mother

The story of Marta unfolded in the scenic, passionate heart of Valdagno, northeast Italy. Born on a warm August day in 1964, her early life was steeped in the charming, predictable cadence of traditional Italian ethos — a stark, structured counterpoint to the high-spirited, eclectic life she was destined to lead. But a deep, unquiet artistic yearning pulsed within her. On her eighteenth birthday, she made her dramatic escape, leaving the comfort of home to chase her aspirations across the wide canvas of Europe.

For six years, she was a cultural nomad, allowing the diversity of the continent to enrich her soul and deepen the hues of her art. Then, in 1989, a call from a new friend changed everything. She described an enchanting island where creativity didn't just flourish but pulsed in the air. Drawn by this vivid image, Marta found herself stepping onto the shores of Bali.

It was here that she met Shane, an Australian artist, and their shared obsession with creation quickly ignited a partnership that was both romantic and intensely creative. Their joint artwork rapidly became a talking point among the local expatriate community. Shane, a visionary in his own right, was collaborating with John on the custom furniture destined for his unique wooden houses. It was through this connection that Marta's path finally converged with John's.

The connection was immediate — a profound jolt of recognition. Fate seemed to have drawn its own bold design, and they embarked on a new, limitless journey filled with creativity and love. Marta was a figure of luminosity, a ray of light. Friends and family still recall how her pure openness and exuberant spontaneity injected a unique, unforgettable vibrancy into every space she entered. She was not only an accomplished abstract painter but also an expressive pianist, her paintings telling vivid stories and her fingers pulling melodic narratives from the keys. Her beauty was radiant, not merely skin-deep, but housed in a generous smile that reached her eyes, radiating an aura of positivity that transformed any room into a haven of warmth and joy.

John, recognizing the sacred nature of her talent, presented her with a grand piano, a gesture that symbolized his unwavering support for her artistic soul. Within the expansive haven of his home — a sanctuary John purposely kept open for other creative spirits — Marta found the freedom to fully express herself, her personality woven into every piece of art and every echoed melody. They became co-creators in an imaginative world, Marta's artistic mind perfectly balanced by John's dreamer's vision.

In 1990, the delicate balance of their world was brutally disrupted. During a routine visa run to Singapore, the simple act of eating an apple led to a life-threatening illness: a severe bacterial infection called leptospirosis. While she eventually recovered from the physical infection, it sparked something else: she began to exhibit signs of a split personality.

It was a stark, cold reminder of life's fragility, but Marta's spirit was indefatigable. Concerned for her well-being, John reached out to her family, seeking an explanation for these sudden psychological changes. Despite their firm assurances that there was no history of mental health issues, John's instinct persisted, leading him to suggest a psychological evaluation back in Singapore. She clung to life and survived the ordeal.

Months after her return, life blossomed anew with the news of her pregnancy. However, this joy was soon clouded by a growing, unsettling concern. John noticed a subtle but disturbing shift in Marta's demeanor and moods.

The diagnosis was a seismic revelation: bipolar disorder. It posed an immediate, life-altering challenge, particularly the suggestion of medicinal intervention. Marta, standing firm in her self-belief and conviction, resolutely chose to navigate the tempest without medication. Their return to Bali brought a fragile semblance of normalcy, a life filled by the warm current of their love and creativity. But beneath the surface, the silent, unpredictable struggle of the human mind remained.

During the ebb and flow of this tested bond, I arrived on April 15, 1991, wrapped in warmth and affection. In the months that followed, Marta's spirit, far from broken, revealed its relentless energy. Harnessing the creative explosion inspired by motherhood, she debuted her first art exhibition on August 10, 1991. The event was not merely a display of her artistic prowess; it was a defiant celebration of her journey, a manifestation of her freedom to create. Surrounded by the love and support of her inner circle, Marta's exhibition was a resounding success. Every single piece of her dynamic artwork found a new home, a tangible testament to the profound impact of her talent and vision. She was living the dreams she had nurtured, embracing the freedom she had chased across continents, and basking in a collage of happiness and contentment. In that period, every possibility felt within reach, and every day was a brilliant celebration of art, love, and the new life they had created together.

The journey of life, often a complex blend of brilliance and shadow, brought unforeseen and devastating change. The unspoken pain that Marta wrestled with was a sorrow more profound than anyone grasped. The passionate ideas and dreams she had so freely shared were slowly, silently overshadowed by an inner turmoil, a battle largely invisible to the world outside her bright, creative facade. It is a chilling reminder that behind the most lively of surfaces, a hidden darkness can lie, often overlooked until the final moment.

On March 1, 1993, John's world was irrevocably shattered. He found Marta dead in his mother's small granny flat, tucked away within the family compound on the edge of the property. She had hanged herself. The sight of her — the woman he loved, the mother of his child — dangling in that quiet room was a shock that defied logic. John didn't hesitate; he rushed to her, his hands fumbling and shaking as he fought to untie the rope. He lowered her to the floor, his heart hammering against his ribs as he tried to find a pulse, a breath, anything.

"Call an ambulance!" he screamed. "Berate, call an ambulance!"

Berate followed the sound of his shouting and found them there on the floor. Together, they tried everything they could to bring her back, but the room remained hauntingly still.

In the hollow silence that followed, John's protective instincts took over. He told Berate to leave the house before the police arrived. He didn't want her or the staff subjected to the suspicion and relentless questioning that follow an unexplained death. Even in his shattered state, he had the presence of mind to try and shield them from the maze of the Indonesian bureaucracy — a system he knew could be cold and unforgiving to those caught in its gears.

But there was no shielding himself. In the weeks that followed, the man Berate knew seemed to vanish. He became a shadow of himself — quieter, heavier, and profoundly lost. He spent his days drifting through a haze of beer, not out of a desire to drink, but because the weight of the silence was too much to bear sober. Marta never left a reason why, leaving John to live in the permanent "after" of a question that would never be answered.

> *What life takes with one hand,*
> *it sometimes gives with another.*

Silvia, My Stepmother

We turn now to the captivating journey of Silvia, a woman who, like Marta, was drawn by a magnetic pull of love and discovery to the enchanting shores of Bali. With her bright, vivacious personality and a humor that was infectious, she not only found love but became a truly delightful presence in my life. She is, perhaps in a reflection of my father's complicated history, my only official stepmother.

Silvia was an Italian teacher whose musical talents enabled her to teach the piano as well. She possessed an innate sense of adventure; an eagerness to chase the unknown. Her first arrival in Bali was in 1992 at the invitation of friends who recognized her zest for life and curiosity about the island's unique blend of culture, art, and natural beauty. During that first visit, she had a fleeting, utterly unremarkable encounter with John, Marta, and myself, then just a baby — none of us aware of the profound, destiny-altering role she would soon play.

Over the following years, Silvia's trips to the island grew more frequent, each visit strengthening the invisible bond with John and his family. They eventually married in a beautiful, traditional Balinese ceremony in 1997. Then, in 1999, answering the definitive call of her heart, she made a life-changing decision: she resigned from her teaching post in Italy and moved to Bali permanently, taking up residence with John in his Legian house.

Silvia's arrival as the third stepmother marked a new, energetic chapter in our home. Her laughter was infectious, her lightheartedness a welcome force, and her uncanny ability to find humor in the mundane brought a refreshing, vital energy. She filled the house with a renewed happiness, turning every room into a playground. There were constant games of hide-and-seek, and I loved the way her laugh would ring out the moment we caught one another - a sound

that made the house feel truly alive. Her story beauti-
fully illustrates how the meandering, unexpected
paths of life can ultimately lead us to the most joyful
new beginnings.

> *Each family is a universe, with stars of love and comets of challenge that orbit the heart's persistent pull.*

Reflections on Resilience and the Cycle of Life

John's journey is a testament to the strength found in resilience, adaptability, and an unyielding belief in oneself. From his early days, faced with the need to carve out his own path, John learned to adapt, embrace change, and find opportunities in unexpected places. His story shows that life isn't a straight line; it's a winding path, sometimes filled with more questions than answers. It is in moments of uncertainty that we often discover our greatest strengths and deepest insights.

Throughout his life, John faced challenges that could have easily held him back, but instead, he saw them as opportunities to learn, grow, and explore new directions. In his youth, he learned the value of hard work, realizing that success was something he had to create rather than inherit. As he navigated the demands of adulthood, each challenge prepared him for the next, helping him build resilience along the way. His journey wasn't about perfection; it was about persistence — showing up and giving his best despite the odds.

Life doesn't come with a map, and often the path we start on isn't the one we stay on. Sometimes we take detours and sometimes we're forced to rebuild. Like John, we each encounter moments when we must adapt, let go of what we thought life would look like, and embrace what it is becoming. These moments shape us, teaching us about ourselves and showing us that even when things fall apart, we can learn and grow with resilience, knowing we have the capacity to rebuild after each crisis.

John's journey also highlights the importance of relationships. Along his path, he met people who challenged him, taught him, and believed in him. Above all, he believed in himself. Relationships became both anchors and catalysts for his growth, reminding him that even the most independent journeys require connection. His journey invites us to reflect on our own relationships and to value the people who support and challenge us along the way.

Life is an ever-evolving cycle of beginnings and endings. Just as in nature, where seasons change and trees shed their leaves only to bloom again, we experience cycles of loss, renewal, and transformation. When we lose something — whether it's a relationship, an opportunity, or a sense of stability — it creates space for something new to take its place. This isn't always easy to recognize in the moment, but with time, we often see how our losses lead to growth, new connections, or unforeseen opportunities. Much like the passing seasons, once one season ends, another is on its way.

Our past is the foundation on which the present is built. Every experience, loss, and success shapes the person we are today. Even when we fall, those moments create fertile ground for renewal, much like how a tree's fallen leaves nourish the soil for future growth. Understanding that life moves in cycles helps us accept change and recognize that each fall is not the end but the beginning of something new. Every fall is an opportunity to grow, build resilience, and develop character. We pave our own path by using our past experiences as lessons to shape the future we desire.

CHAPTER II

Embracing the Culture and Relationships That Shape Us

Berate, My Balinese Mom

Melody Beattie wrote, "Every person we meet writes a line in the story of our lives — some with ink that fades quickly, others with marks that shape entire chapters." One of those lasting marks came from a woman named Nyoman Berate.

Berate entered the world in December of 1963, a time when the very soul of the island was trembling. Born in the shadow of Mount Agung's devastating eruption, her life was destined to be bound to the spirit of renewal. Her family owned little, but their true wealth lay in their deep-seated resilience. They occupied a modest home offered by the village priest, nestled within the temple grounds of Tianyar on Mount Agung's northern slope.

At the tender age of six, her world suffered its own seismic event. A faint, harmless tremor from the volcano — a sound that carried the heavy memory of the 1963 trauma — triggered a fatal heart attack in her mother, who had never fully healed from the eruption's psychological toll. Childhood ended abruptly, and responsibility became her fierce, unforgiving tutor. While other children played, Berate was at the local market selling rice, livestock, and produce to secure her family's survival. She counted coins, bartered with neighbors, and acquired the quiet, formidable strength that ripens the heart long before its time.

Her father eventually remarried, introducing a stepmother and younger stepbrother. From this new matriarch, Berate absorbed the intricate domestic arts of Balinese cooking and household care, as was customary. Though she never attended school, her days became a classroom of their own. The market taught her endurance and her family taught her patience, compassion, and adaptability — qualities that would define her character.

By 1977, a turning point emerged. At fifteen, Berate accepted an invitation to work for her relative, Asti, as a helping hand to his family. At the time, Asti owned a garment business in Kuta. The bustling town was a world apart from her village life, full of opportunity and energy. It was also where her path would first cross with John, a business acquaintance of Asti who would later play a significant role in her life. Their early encounters were brief, but the seeds of connection were quietly sown.

In 1981, at just seventeen, Berate met and married Nyoman Dayuh, affectionately nicknamed Unyil, meaning "short person" in Balinese. Dayuh, twenty-five and from Tianyar, shared her hopes and dreams, and the couple settled into a small rental unit within a Balinese family compound in Legian. Their space was tiny — three by three meters — with a shared squat toilet and a bucket shower. Resourceful as they were, they set up a makeshift kitchen at the unit's remaining space in front of the unit door. Dayuh took on various jobs, from selling bus tickets to working at a nearby vehicle rental company, while Berate embraced her responsibilities caring for Asti's children.

Life brought both joy and sorrow. Shortly after their marriage, Berate gave birth to a daughter, who fell ill and passed away within months. Grieving but resilient, Berate and Dayuh hoped for a child again, and in 1982, welcomed a healthy son, Made. That same year, seeking further opportunity, Berate approached John for employment. Recognizing the quiet dignity and diligence that radiated from her, he offered her a position as a housekeeper in his Legian home. This role marked the beginning of a new chapter, opening doors that would eventually shape her life in profound ways.

In 1983, Berate and Dayuh welcomed their second son, Komang. With no local kindergarten, her two boys became fixtures at John's residence, accompanying her to work each day. Over time, John's home transformed into a makeshift kindergarten, providing a safe and nurturing space not only for Made and Komang but also for neighboring children. The large garden became a playground, alive with laughter and activity, reflecting the communal spirit central to Balinese culture.

As Made and Komang grew, John's commitment deepened: he financed their education through high school. Berate's role profoundly transcended that of a housekeeper. She became a constant, indispensable presence in his life, and in time, her world and John's became inseparable, bound by shared years, laughter, and the quiet understanding that family is a connection forged by presence, not just blood. Berate was the unwavering cornerstone of our household, quietly shaping the lives of all around her — including mine.

Early Balinese Upbringing

> *Every new beginning comes from some other beginning's end — Lucius Annaeus Seneca*

As I begin to share the intricacies of my Balinese upbringing, I navigate a story rich with family, culture, and the unique bonds that define who we are. Within these pages, I've outlined the roles of those who shaped my early years — referring to John and Marta as my birth parents, while Berate and her husband, Nyoman, became my "mom" and "dad" in the heart of Bali. Though simple in wording, this distinction carries the depth of the sea, encapsulating a story of love, belonging, and the delicate dance of relationships that has formed the melody of my life.

From the moment I entered this world, Berate transcended her role as a nanny and housekeeper, becoming the anchor in the ever-shifting tides of my infancy. The transformation in our relationship wasn't marked by grand gestures but by quiet, everyday moments of care and understanding. As a relentlessly crying newborn, I seemed to find peace only in her arms. Those first whispers of comfort became the beginning of a bond that would go on to define my understanding of family.

This unique comfort I found with Berate led to a shift in our daily lives. My parents, John and Marta, weary from sleepless nights and Marta's fragile health, began to notice a pattern with each sunrise: my cries faded the moment Berate arrived. What began as relief gradually reshaped the pulse of our lives, and Berate's role evolved into something far more profound than any title could convey.

The depth of this connection became particularly evident when Berate recently shared with me her reflections on those early days, revealing the natural peace that enveloped me in her care. "When I gave

you back to your mom, you wouldn't stop crying —
but with me, you found peace," she said softly. That
peace became the foundation of an arrangement that
grew naturally. I began spending more time in the
nurture of Berate's family, where affection and stability replaced the restlessness of infancy. Seeing the
bond we shared, and concerned for both Marta's
well-being and my own, John and Marta made the
heartfelt decision to entrust my care to Berate day and
night.

When Berate's family became my own, the lines
of family were drawn not by blood but by the enduring connections of the heart. In her home, I was not
merely a child under her care — I was a cherished
member of the family, and she nurtured me with the
same love and warmth as her own sons. This transition marked the beginning of an upbringing steeped
in the values, traditions, and communal spirit of Bali.

A pivotal moment further cemented Berate's role
in my life. Following Marta's untimely passing on
March 1, 1993, the fabric of our family shifted irrevocably. With a heart as vast as the Balinese sky, Berate
stepped fully into the role of mother as naturally as
she had with her own sons.

As I reflect now, I can only assume why John
made the choice he did. He faced the reality that his
ability to care for me, shaped by his own childhood
experiences, was limited. Therefore, his decision came
from love and practicality: he recognized that he

could not fully offer Berate's care, stability, warmth, and guidance, so he allowed me to remain where I would thrive. It was a decision born not from absence of love, but from its quiet abundance, a recognition of where my well-being truly lay. I am filled with gratitude for John's decisions and for the immense love and care Berate gave me, wrapping me in the warmth of a family that transcended conventional definitions.

As time unfolded its wings, quietly carrying me past the age of six, our living arrangements in Legian remained largely the same, though sharing a double bed among the five of us became a growing challenge. In true Balinese fashion, we adapted, finding comfort in the cool shelter of the ceramic floor on sweltering nights. We hardly noticed the absence of a fan until a few years later, when, presumably, funds allowed its purchase — a small marker of our simple way of living. Tropical nights required closed windows and doors to keep mosquitoes at bay, while rats and cockroaches roamed around us as if the place were theirs too. Occasionally, one of us would wake up screaming, frantically trying to kill a pest that had crawled too close. Unyil, ever resourceful, often sought the relative cool of the outdoors because the room often became unbearably hot with all of us crammed inside.

An intriguing aspect of Balinese culture shaped our nightly rituals, one of which was the practice of sleeping with the lights on, a safeguard against unseen spirits that roam the night. This tradition, so ingrained in my daily life, made darkness feel foreign. Sleeping bathed in light was as natural to me as breathing, reflecting a childhood seamlessly intertwined with the customs and beliefs of Bali. These early years were foundational, shaping the person I would become — a soul forever connected to Balinese culture and the family that had cared for me as their own.

Tucked within the heart of our living quarters were three units, including ours, each sharing the land with the landlord's main family home. These spaces became stages upon which the diverse tapestry of Indonesian life played out before my young eyes. Over the years, a revolving door of families and individuals from across Indonesia passed through, many leaving not by choice but due to relentless economic pressures that made sustaining the rent too great a challenge.

In this communal living environment, secrets were as rare as a cool breeze during the dry season. Information flowed freely, much like the rapid exchange we now associate with the internet. This openness reflected the Balinese ethos of sharing, a cultural cornerstone that nurtured a profound sense of community and interconnectedness.

The closely packed layout of our home, with neighboring units pressed against ours, created a living environment where boundaries were fluid and doors stood open. Life flowed seamlessly from one home to the next, fostering friendships that grew naturally among the children. These bonds were born not just from circumstance but from shared experiences, trust, and understanding, and many of them endured into adulthood, anchoring me to a community as integral to my identity as my own family.

My early years were shaped by this spirit of openness, generosity, and connection — a celebration of the Balinese way of life. Growing up in such a nurturing environment, where every interaction carried the warmth of kinship, left an indelible mark on me. It shaped my understanding of family, friendship, and the intricate web of relationships that binds all together.

Daily Life

> *Every routine day stacks up to build a lifetime of unexpected wisdom and subtle strengths.*

Life in our compound, shaped by community and care, moved in harmony with the flow of each day. Growing up in this environment meant that the ordinary routines of daily life were anything but mundane; they were rich with lessons, subtle wisdom, and the values of Balinese culture that went far beyond the surface.

Among these daily practices was Berate's predawn journey to the local market, a ritual that governed the household's rhythm. At 4:30 a.m., as the world whispered in the quiet hours of night transitioning to day, Berate would venture out on foot to gather the day's sustenance. She returned sometime later, carrying two or three large, red plastic bags brimming with the freshest groceries, a signal that the day of culinary magic and communal joy was about to begin.

As dawn approached, Berate's morning ritual of love and care was already underway. By the time the first light brushed the sky at 5.30 a.m., the chickens clucked their natural alarm, and the air carried the aroma of a freshly prepared feast, signaling the start of another day in our shared life.

Berate's morning ritual of cooking a large meal for the family was an act of love that transcended mere nutrition. She would cook one meal each day that served as breakfast, lunch, and dinner, with dishes inspired by the market's offerings and elevated by her creativity. The simplicity of the food belied its rich and complex flavors — flavors that are nearly impossible to capture in words. Each dish, though seemingly straightforward, was a delicate exploration of taste, delighting the senses while nourishing the soul.

Our kitchen, if it could be called that, was nothing more than a small table and stove positioned by the unit entrance door. Yet every morning, it became the heart of our home. Berate transformed simple ingredients into extraordinary meals, filling the air with aromas that served as the day's most effective alarm clock. Each day brought a different fragrance; sometimes the day's catch was paired with rice and vegetables, steamed in a bamboo funnel, with fish seasoned in Berate's special blend of spices, and wrapped in banana leaves. The method infused the fish with the aroma of spices and leaves while imparting a subtle smokiness to the rice, turning humble ingredients into a symphony of flavors.

In our home, utensils, chairs, and tables were absent from our dining rituals. We ate wherever we could find space, holding our plates in one hand while using the other to enjoy the food. In keeping with tradition, we ate with our hands, a practice that, almost magically, seemed to amplify the flavors of Berate's cooking. This tactile connection to our meals created an intimate dance of texture, warmth, and taste, bringing each dish vividly to life.

Each meal Berate cooked was a daily blessing, a ritual that combined food, love, and prayer. Through this simple yet profound act, she taught us the essence of Balinese life: every meal a celebration, every bite a prayer, and every day a gift to be cherished with gratitude and joy.

Berate fed me by her own hand until I was about five years old, each morsel infused with care and tradition. While some might see this as spoiling, it was deeply rooted in our culture; a tactile expression of love and nurturing that went far beyond mere sustenance. This practice embodied the heart of Balinese family life, where feeding a child by hand was a sacred ritual that bonded us from the earliest age. It wasn't a reflection of our inability to feed ourselves, but a conscious cultural choice, wrapping every meal in significance, affection, and connection.

After our communal breakfast, the tempo of the morning shifted toward cleanliness — another collective ritual shaped by our shared living arrangements. The three units shared a single shower, and so began the familiar morning line. We shared a small bucket filled with our family's mix of essentials — soap, shampoo, toothbrushes, all jumbled together in one humble container. The shower itself offered no luxury — no hot water, just a cool cascade drawn from a communal tank. Each scoop of water struck the skin with a sharp wakefulness, washing away the last remnants of sleep. My brother and I often showered together, laughing as we took turns scooping water from the tank and pouring it over each other's heads, with the unspoken understanding that these simple routines stitched us together in ways comfort never could.

Dressed and groomed by my older brothers, I emerged into the day with a sense of pride and readiness — a reflection of Berate's quiet insistence that we face the world with dignity, no matter how modest our means. Then, in a familiar procession that echoed the steady flow of island life, Berate led us on a short walk to John's house. Her bags, once heavy with breakfast ingredients, were now repacked with supplies for her day's work.

John's lush garden became our playground, a living canvas of green where imagination bloomed freely. Beneath the canopy of frangipani and mango trees, we built kingdoms, forged adventures, and lost ourselves in the untamed natural beauty that surrounded us. The world felt infinite there, as though the garden itself breathed life into our games.

Language, too, shaped the landscape of my early life. I spoke only Balinese then — each word, phrase, and inflection steeped in the flow of the island and the warmth of the people who raised me. My language carried the scent of Berate's cooking, the laughter of our shared shower, and the gentle hum of daily life beneath the tropical sun. Those words became my first home, a living link to the love, labor, and lessons that defined my earliest years — a childhood lived between worlds, yet belonging completely to both.

Berate's responsibilities extended far beyond our morning rituals. Within John's household, she was the heartbeat that kept everything in motion — cleaning, making beds, hand-washing endless cycles of manual laundry long before the hum of washing machines found their way to Bali, and preparing elaborate local lunch dishes for John and his many guests. Each day unfolded like a ceremony of care and endurance. Despite the demands, Berate met every task with grace, her strength quiet but unyielding and her spirit infused into every corner of that home.

At five o'clock, when the workday ended, my dad would pick us up on his scooter and drive us home. The best part of the day was the daily afternoon ritual with him. We would sit at the roadside of our complex and watch the world go by, locals stopping for a quick chat. I would sit listening to the occasional puzzling foreign interaction, not understanding a word, and Dad would offer a polite wave to the ladies who drove past.

It was during these regular afternoons that my dad introduced me to Coca-Cola. We'd buy it from the local *warung* where, as was the custom, they'd pour the soda into a small plastic bag and keep the glass bottle for reuse. My dad would shake the bag vigorously to release the fizz, and then we'd drink the chilled cola together. This was more than just a drink on the curb side — this simple shared experience was a moment of deep bonding with my dad that I have cherished ever since.

But those quiet afternoons were only part of the rhythm of our home. My mother's presence set the true cadence, and her resilience shone brightest on the rare occasions when illness overtook her. Those days were the quietest in our home, when the absence of her cooking left an emptiness that could almost be heard. Without the familiar scent of her magical spices drifting through the air, the house seemed to pause, holding its breath. On those rare days, we would venture out for food — simple dishes from nearby *warungs* or Chinese stalls — each bite a small adventure into flavors that felt foreign yet curiously comforting. Still, even when weariness pulled at her body at times, Berate refused to let us go hungry. She would summon her remaining strength to prepare something quick and humble — instant noodles, perhaps, or a simple rice dish — meals that carried the same quiet love as her grander feasts.

Her perseverance, even when her body longed for rest, was a lesson far deeper than words could teach. In her steadfastness, I learned what true devotion looked like — not the loud kind proclaimed with effort, but the silent kind lived through every small act of care.

Looking back through the lens of her stories, those she shares softly now, in the twilight of her years, I see more than the rhythm of her days. I see the strength behind them. Her life, threaded with joy, fatigue, laughter, and sacrifice, painted the portrait of a woman whose love anchored our world. The stories alone could never capture all she gave, yet they offer a glimpse into her immense heart. Berate's legacy lives not just in memory, but in the way we move through life — in how we love, work, and give of ourselves. It is her quiet power, her enduring grace, that continues to shape who we have become and all that we have learned about family love.

John's Home

In the memories that shape my childhood story, "John's Home" occupies a chapter filled with wonder, adventure, and the discovery of worlds both familiar and foreign. If our modest compound was the heart of our daily life, then John's home was its counterpart. It was here that the rhythms of my two worlds intertwined — the humble simplicity of Balinese living and the quiet sophistication of my father's life.

Berate, my mother in spirit, whom I still lovingly call *Mom* — introduced me to this haven, which also happened to be my biological father's home and her place of work. Unbeknownst to me, those long hours I spent there from Monday to Saturday, playing beneath the shade of towering trees and wandering through its gardens, were shaping the foundations of who I truly belong to.

The garden, a sprawling paradise I fondly called *the big jungle,* was tended by Wayan, the patient gardener who single-handedly kept this slice of heaven alive. Built of bamboo and straw, John's home stood open to the world — no fences, no walls — just the seamless invitation of nature itself. The neighboring children and I would run freely through the property, our laughter echoing through the greenery. I was the bold one, climbing trees, playing near the small fires set by Wayan, the gardener, to burn dry leaves, or laying on the pile of hay only to get itchy afterwards.

This garden wasn't just a playground; it was a living pantry. We feasted on mangoes, *jewetan* (a Balinese fruit), and the spiky sweetness of hairy lychee fruits that ripened with the seasons. Each fruit carried the taste of sweet freedom — sticky fingers, wide smiles, and the kind of joy that can only be found in childhood.

It was in that garden that I first encountered the word *tourist.* I didn't yet understand what it meant, only that it described the curious strangers who visited John's home. Their attempts to speak with me were met with my playful confusion and a mischievous Balinese grin.

"Hey, tourist!" I would shout at John, unaware that this teasing phrase would one day come to symbolize the bridge between my two worlds — the "Balinese child" and the son of an Australian father.

Among the laughter and games, something deeper was taking root. The English words I overheard from John's guests slowly began to take shape in my mind, mixing with my native tongue like colors blending on a canvas. Without realizing it, those playful days became the beginning of my journey into bilingualism — a subtle education that emerged not from books, but from the everyday influences of John's guests.

During one of those carefree afternoons, when the garden hummed with laughter and the air was thick with adventure, two figures appeared at the edge of my world — a white man and woman whose faces were foreign to me. Their approach was gentle, but to my untamed spirit, it felt like an intrusion into the wild sanctuary that was mine alone.

I was accustomed to the warm familiarity of Jean, John's mother, who often visited bearing chocolates and soft koala teddies. But these two strangers were different. Their closeness, their unreadable smiles, and their unknown intentions unsettled me. In a world where I roamed free and fearless, their presence felt like a quiet storm on the horizon.

Before reason could catch up with instinct, my small hands reached for the nearest thing within grasp — a heavy C4 battery. Its weight was solid, almost comforting, as fear surged through me. Without hesitation, I hurled it toward the man. The battery struck his head with startling precision, the sound of its impact breaking the stillness like a crack of thunder. For a fleeting moment, the world froze. I stared, heart pounding, as a thin line of red appeared on his scalp. The rush of defiance ebbed, replaced by a dawning sense of confusion and the first flicker of remorse.

Only years later did I come to understand the truth of that day. The man and woman I had mistaken for intruders were not strangers at all; they were my grandparents, who had travelled all the way from Italy to meet their grandchild for the first time. What unfolded in that instant was more than an accident, it was a collision of unknown worlds. My free-spirited, barefoot life in Bali had met, with shocking force, the foreign world of family I had never known.

Prayers

> *Sacred moments hide in ordinary days.*

In my upbringing, the practice of prayer was a cornerstone of daily life, intricately tied to the rich fabric of Hindu culture that enveloped our existence. The ritual of praying three times a day — morning, midday, and afternoon — was not merely a routine but a sacred tradition, an acknowledgment of the unseen forces that guide and protect us. It was a practice steeped in respect and gratitude, where we offered tokens of beauty and sweetness — flowers, fruits, cookies, or candies — coupled with the hypnotic fragrance of frangipani incense to honor the ancestral spirits that watched over us. These offerings found their places in the sanctuaries of our home: the temple, the entrance, the kitchen, and the bedroom temple, each space reflecting our reverence for the divine and the protective spirits of our ancestors.

As a child, the nuances of prayer were not taught to me through formal instruction but were observed through the actions of those around me. I learned not through words but by witnessing the silent devotion of my family, emulating the hand gestures that accompanied the placement of offerings. My understanding of prayer was instinctual, a mimicry born of a desire to participate in this dance of spirit and matter. To my young mind, prayer was less about articulation and more about maintaining a harmonious balance with the unseen world, a barter of sorts to ensure peace and prevent mischief from the spiritual realm.

It was only as I grew older, stepping into the wider circles of community and ceremony, that the layers of this tradition began to unfold before me. I gradually became acquainted with mantras, the act of asking, and most importantly, the quiet grace of praying not just for oneself but for others. With age came the understanding of a profound principle underpinning Hinduism — the law of balance. This realization illuminated the depth of our daily rituals, revealing prayer as something far greater than habit or superstition. It was a practice that touched the very essence of cosmic harmony.

This evolution of understanding — from the innocent mimicry of childhood to a deeper awareness of spiritual equilibrium — mirrored my own journey from seeing prayer as a safeguard to recognizing it as a way of being. It reflected the Hindu belief in a universe held together by balance, where every offering, every mantra, contributes to the harmony between the seen and unseen worlds. In this growing awareness, I came to understand prayer not merely as a path to peace, but as a living expression of interconnectedness — a dialogue with the divine that nourishes the soul and binds us, all of us, into one continuous thread of existence.

Downtime

> *In the quiet moments of the evening, the television was not just an appliance, but a window to worlds beyond our own.*

Throughout my childhood in Balinese culture, Hindu prayers, and the untamed freedom of John's garden, moments of tranquility and routine marked the close of each day. As the sun dipped below the horizon, these rare and cherished moments unfolded in the evenings, a sacred time that belonged to my Balinese mom and dad. Their indulgence, a simple yet profound pleasure, was immersing themselves in the dramatic and colorful world of an Indian Bollywood TV series. Each evening, as the clock struck 6 p.m., our home transformed into a mini cinema, the television screen alight with the spectacle of Bollywood drama that captivated our hearts.

The show itself was a mere half-hour journey into stories of love, conflict, and resolution, but frequent interruptions for advertisements stretched the experience to a full hour. This ritual, punctuated by commercial breaks, allowed us a glimpse into another world rich with emotion and the vibrancy of Indian culture. Once the credits rolled and the final ad played, the baton was passed to us kids. Eagerly, we seized control of the television, flipping the channel to dive into the world of American action movies. The allure wasn't in the narrative, which often eluded our grasp due to the language barrier, but in the spectacle of action and adventure that transcended words. In the glow of the TV screen, we unwittingly expanded our linguistic horizons, picking up English words and phrases that we later paraded with pride and a hint of mischief on the streets, oblivious to their meanings but delighted by the sounds.

In our household, the concept of a fixed bedtime was as foreign as the English language. We surrendered to sleep on our own terms, only when weariness claimed us. Many nights, the television continued to whisper into the darkness, a low-volume guardian against the silence, while the lights stood vigilant. This combination of flickering images and soft illumination served as our nightly sentinel, providing a comforting backdrop to our slumber. In these moments of shared stillness, with Bollywood dramas fading into American action sequences, the day gently receded, leaving behind a sense of security and belonging that cradled us until morning's light.

Weekends

In the rhythm of our lives, Saturdays blended into the routine of work and school, while Sundays carved out a distinct space for leisure and communal gathering. There was the anticipation of rare treats, like the two-cent jelly cakes that Mom always made on Sundays. Our neighborhood would come alive in our landlord's common area, a vibrant hub where everyone gathered for long rounds of card games or the rowdy spectacle of *tajen*. But beneath the surface of the gambling — now technically illegal — lies an ancient ritual: the religious rite of *Tabuh Rah*. This "spilling of blood" is a sacred sacrifice, a ritual meant to purify the earth and appease the restless spirits of the unseen world. The air was always thick with anticipation, camaraderie, and laughter. Those games carried on until the wallets were finally lightened.

For us children, Sundays brought a unique kind of excitement. Our eyes were not fixed on the domino card games but on the traveling salesmen and women who meandered through our gatherings. They brought with them an array of temptations — cigarettes for the adults, snacks, and premium products not found in our regular *warungs*. These vendors, aware of the Sunday routine, timed their visits to coincide with the gambling, knowing their treats were more tempting against the backdrop of a leisurely gamble.

The possibility of indulging in these coveted goodies hinged on the fortunes of the day's bets. Our anticipation was a gamble in itself, with our hopes pinned on the success of my mom or dad at the table. The salespeople, with their baskets of goods, became figures of keen interest for me, not just for their wares but for their curiosity toward me.

"Heh! A white boy, speaking Balinese!" he exclaimed, his eyes wide with confusion. "I have lived here five years and still my tongue trips over these words, yet you speak like you were born in the village dust," he added.

This piqued their interest and often led them to linger longer than usual. Coming from neighboring islands where the native language was Javanese and job opportunities were scarce, their command of Balinese was not as fluent, making my seamless integration into the local dialect a subject of fascination.

The Funny Story of Coffee

*During the innocence of childhood,
every flavor can taste like magic
and every belief can hold a universe
of possibilities.*

This story from my life, bridging my Balinese up-bringing and the wider world, encapsulates the curious blend of imagination and the earnest desires of a young heart, marked by the innocent misconceptions and simple joys of childhood.

As the years added layers to my understanding and experience, one daily ritual in our household caught my attention and sparked a peculiar notion within my young mind. Each morning, my Balinese parents would partake in a ritual that involved a dark, aromatic liquid that filled the air with its inviting scent. This drink, which I came to know was coffee, seemed to hold a magical property in my eyes. Observing the dark tresses of my parents and local friends, I concocted a whimsical theory: perhaps drinking this black beverage could transform my blond hair to match the raven locks of those around me. My underlying desire was to weave myself more deeply into the fabric of the community and family that had embraced me.

My initial foray into the world of coffee was driven by this innocent wish, but it quickly turned into a love affair with the drink itself. The coffee, sweetened to appeal to a child's palate, was like a warm, sugary embrace with a hint of exotic spice, a concoction that won my heart at first sip. Yet, when I voiced my hope that continued indulgence in this black drink would darken my hair and further blend me into the family, the response was an uproar of laughter. My Balinese parents and brothers found my earnest belief both endearing and amusing.

Going to Balinese School

> *The lessons learned on the playgrounds of our youth are those that shape our understanding of friendship, competition, and the value of diverse voices.*

At six years old, with my limited English proficiency, I was enrolled in a local kindergarten in Legian just a stone's throw from John's residence. John's own educational experiences had left him with a deep-seated aversion to formal schooling.

At this school, nestled within the vibrant community of Legian, I stood out as the only white student. However, my unique position never felt isolating. Having been immersed in the heart of Balinese culture from birth, I was not just known as John's son but also recognized for my deep-rooted integration into the local way of life, speaking Balinese fluently and living under Berate's nurturing care.

My days at school mirrored those of my peers. Berate, embodying the roles of both parent and guardian, ensured my timely arrival and departure each day. Within the school's walls, I was no different from my classmates. We shared meals, language, laughter, and games. The camaraderie and acceptance I experienced were profound; my peers saw me not as an outsider, but as one of their own — a brother in play and daily life. We sat in the dirt and ate with our bare hands, sharing sweet drinks poured into plastic takeaway bags. To my friends, I was just another one of the boys, my pale skin invisible to them as we roamed the streets. It was only when we passed the local shops that the "outsider" label returned; shopkeepers would freeze, stunned, calling out to my group, "Who is that white kid?" But my peers never skipped a beat.

Without hesitation, they would answer, "He's our friend."

To them, I wasn't a *bule*; I was simply one of the pack.

I navigated my school days with a sense of belonging and identity that transcended the superficial differences in appearance. In this nurturing environment, I was an integral part of a collective; a young soul growing and learning in harmony with the effervescent culture that had embraced me since my earliest days.

My memories of those school mornings are as vivid as if they were just yesterday. Made and Komang, my Balinese brothers who were a few years my senior, played a pivotal role in my daily routine. They would meticulously comb my hair to the side, applying gel to achieve a look that was very fashionable at the time. Our school attire was quite formal — shirts and blazers, complete with ties and belts cinching our shorts, long socks pulled up high, and polished black shoes.

Our mornings were punctuated by a routine steeped in discipline and national pride. At 6 a.m., the school bell summoned us to the grounds for a ceremonial flag-raising, marking the start of our academic day. Dressed in our crisp uniforms, we stood in precise, military-like lines, our voices merging in the solemn strains of the Indonesian anthem, hands saluting the ascending flags.

In the classrooms, Indonesian, the national language, served as the medium of instruction — a language that, despite its official status, felt foreign to the vernacular of our home life. Balinese, the language that resonated through our household conversations, bore little resemblance to Indonesian, presenting a linguistic challenge I gradually overcame. By the time I transitioned to grade one at the age of seven, my proficiency in Indonesian had grown significantly. This journey of linguistic and cultural integration reflected the broader narrative of my upbringing, a life lived at the intersection of diverse cultures, languages, and traditions, all converging to shape the person I was becoming.

Transitioning to grade one marked a significant milestone in my educational journey, filled with autonomy and responsibility. It was a rite of passage, a leap from the cocooned environment of kindergarten to a world that mirrored the complexities of adult life. The freedom to walk to and from school unaccompanied was a thrilling development, symbolizing a step toward independence. I took pride in weaving through the motorbikes, stray hens, and barking street dogs, feeling like a true local. The locals who used to give me funny looks because I didn't fit in now simply nodded as I went by.

"Selaaat pagi!" the local tailor would shout from his porch, mock-saluting me as if I were an officer on a mission rather than a five-year-old with a messy backpack.

Independence was the standard held by the teachers I now faced. They were as highly strung as soldiers waiting for the call to battle, their uniforms and haircuts perfect down to the last detail. Because they stood with such rigid pride, they demanded the same from us. Every morning, we formed a military-style line to salute and sing the Indonesian anthem. We had to be immaculate — not a smudge on our clothes or a foot out of place. If we failed, the discipline was public and swift: a beating to the hand to serve as a warning to others. The teachers were the generals, and we were the soldiers being broken into rank. This form of punishment, meted out for lapses in attention, was a stark reminder of the expectations that now rested on our young shoulders.

I vividly remember one of the teachers we had named Ibu Wayan. Once, she caught a boy chatting to a friend and summoned him to the front of the room. A heavy silence fell over the class; we all knew what was coming. As he reached her desk, she commanded him to place his hands flat on the wood. Then, the sharp crack of her foot-long ruler on his hands echoed against the walls — a sound so loud it vibrated through the entire room. The boy walked back to his seat in a daze, tears tracking through the dust on his cheeks, his face twisted in silent pain.

Amidst these lessons in discipline and independence, grade one also introduced the concept of pocket money, a small yet significant empowerment that allowed me to make my own choices within the school's confines. Each morning, my Balinese mom would hand me red notes — hundred Rupiah bills — that felt like a treasure trove in my pocket. Though modest in value, this money allowed me to indulge in the culinary delights of the school canteen.

With just a few of these notes valued at two cents, I could purchase *nasi jingo,* a savory ensemble of rice, chicken, and vegetables neatly wrapped in a banana leaf, along with an assortment of snacks. The canteen's prices mirrored those of the local market, making my modest budget feel ample. This aspect of school life, the ability to choose and savor these simple treats, was a poignant lesson in value and decision-making, imbuing my school days with a sense of autonomy and the subtle joys of growing up.

One afternoon, my mother appeared at the school gates accompanied by a white woman. My friends crowded around, their eyes darting between the two of them and then to me.

"Who is that?" they whispered, nudging me. Then, with a chorus of giggles, they started guessing.

"That must be your grandma! Is that your grandma?"

Grandma? I thought. I didn't even know what that word meant in that context. The sudden laughter made a hot wave of shyness wash over me. I pulled away, keeping as much distance as I could from the white stranger and pressing myself firmly against the familiar side of my Balinese mother as we walked out of the school grounds.

Not all my childhood memories are filled with joy and innocence. Some carry the weight of lessons learned through actions I wish I could undo. One such indelible memory, a stark departure from the usual playground disputes, involves a classmate and a moment of impulsive retaliation that has lingered in my mind ever since.

On that day, a seemingly mundane incident of a stolen snack escalated beyond a mere tussle over treats. When a girl in my class boldly took a snack from my hand and refused to return it, I was thrust into uncharted emotional territory. Never before had I confronted the feeling of being wronged in such a manner. The injustice of it, trivial as it might seem in the grand scheme of life, ignited a response I had not known I was capable of.

Driven by a sense of violation and perhaps influenced by the disciplinary methods I had witnessed, I reacted not with words but with impulsive physicality that I instantly regretted. Removing my belt, I mimicked the punitive actions of our teachers, striking her on the back. She let out a sharp, startled cry and stumbled forward, her face twisting into a mask of pure shock as she clutched the place where the leather had landed. The other children, who had been laughing and playing nearby, suddenly fell back into a jagged circle, their eyes wide with the thrill and terror of witnessing such a forbidden act. The snack lay forgotten on the ground between us. The commotion quickly drew the attention of a passing teacher, whose shadow fell over me before I could even rebuckle my belt. The repercussion of that action was an immediate and significant self-reckoning.

Years have passed since that day. The girl, now a woman, occasionally crosses my path and with a hint of jest, recalls our "good times." Her words, though

light-hearted, resonate with a deeper acknowledgment of our shared history, a moment that, for better
or worse, forged a bond between us.

The journey home after school was not just a
walk, it was an adventure — a daily ritual. Alongside
my friends, I navigated the familiar streets back to
John's house, each step away from school leading us
toward a brief interlude of freedom before the day's
end. On these walks, a small yet significant pleasure
awaited us at the school *warung* or on the way home,
a delightful beverage concocted from condensed
milk, ice, and a unique seaweed jelly. Packaged in a
transparent plastic bag with a straw, it was a refreshing escape, a favorite treat that became an integral
part of my daily routine.

Our route home meandered past a shop brimming with small wooden art pieces, its inventory often spilling onto the path and tempting us with their
crafted beauty. In moments of childish mischief, we
would surreptitiously take a piece, reveling in the
harmless thrill of our small rebellions. These acts of
petty theft, though trivial, were exhilarating, infusing
our routine with a dash of excitement. However, our
actions were not without consequence. The vigilant
shopkeeper, aware of our antics, would occasionally
stand guard, prompting us to alter our path and skirt
the opposite side of the street to avoid his watchful
eye.

In my early years, the concept of time was not governed by the ticking hands of a clock but by the natural cues of our environment. Sunrise, which graced the sky at around 5:30 a.m., signaled that the day had begun and it was time to prepare for school. Our lives were intricately tied to the rhythm of nature, a way of learning about time that was as organic as it was practical.

One particular morning stands out in my memory, marked by an unusual surge of enthusiasm. For a child who typically viewed school with indifference, this sudden eagerness to attend was out of character. I awoke while it was still dark outside, around 4:30 a.m., long before the school day was set to begin. When I announced my intention to head to school early, my Balinese mom, in the midst of her early cooking rituals, cheerfully asked, "Why so early? Is something special happening at school today?"

"No. I just want to go early," I replied.

She shrugged her shoulders as she cut a piece of fruit, and said, "Okay, be careful. It's still dark outside."

I promised I would and stepped outside, surprised at her willingness to let me venture out alone.

The walk to school, a six-hundred-meter journey, was a path I could tread with my eyes closed, so familiar was I with its every turn and landmark. On that quiet morning, the streets were mine alone, a rare solitude in the usually bustling Legian. As I made my way, the anticipation grew, not for the lessons that awaited, but for the sheer novelty of being the first to arrive, embracing a moment of quiet reflection in the typically lively schoolyard.

This memory, a snapshot of youthful impulsiveness and the simple freedom of a dawn walk, encapsulates my deep connection to the world around me during childhood.

The rhythm of school life was synchronized with the agricultural heartbeat of the community, with classes running from 6 a.m. to noon. This thoughtfully designed schedule allowed children to contribute to their family's farm work in the afternoons, reflecting a time when rice paddies flourished, unspoiled by modern construction.

On that unusually early morning, as I arrived at the school's locked gates, I was surprised by a teacher who suddenly appeared.

"You're too early. You'll have to wait outside,' he said.

I settled in, unfazed by the delay. As the hour passed and the sun climbed higher, my classmates began to trickle in, signaling the start of a typical school day. However, something shifted within me during that solitary wait and I felt as though I had already endured a full day at school. Acting on this whimsical sense of time, I chose to retreat home, stepping back into the quiet of the morning and leaving behind a school day that had barely begun.

My return home was to an empty, unlocked house, reflecting the trust and communal spirit of our neighborhood. My Balinese mom, dad, and brothers were already immersed in their day's activities. The absence of a refrigerator meant that meals were prepared fresh daily, with leftovers serving as subsequent meals, if they lasted. That morning, I found the kitchen table laden with provisions prepared by my mom. Alone, I savored the familiar rice breakfast.

The rest of the morning unfolded in peaceful solitude, a drastic change from the communal buzz of school life. With no concept of time beyond the sun's position, I indulged in the rare luxury of daytime television, a momentary escape into a world beyond the confines of our simple, contented existence. This day, marked by an impromptu deviation from routine, underscored the simplicity and self-guided freedom that characterized my childhood, where the sun was my clock, and my decisions, however whimsical, were mine to make.

My Balinese dad's return home for lunch that day, a bit earlier than usual, unfolded without surprise or reprimand upon finding me there instead of at school. His gentle inquiry, devoid of judgment, was, "Why are you home early, Luca?"

His query was met with my innocent fabrication, "I didn't have school today," which he accepted without question, embodying the trust and leniency characteristic of our familial interactions.

This episode highlights the extreme differences in upbringing across cultures. In a Western context of the 1990s, such a deviation from attending school would likely have been met with concern or disciplinary action. However, in the Balinese setting of my childhood, the concept of formal education was still in its infancy. My Balinese parents, having never experienced schooling themselves, navigated this new educational landscape alongside their children, learning its significance and structure in real time.

Schooling was an institution they respected but did not fully comprehend. This disconnect extended to academic support at home; terms like "homework" were foreign concepts, leaving my siblings and me to tackle our educational challenges independently.

The only parental stipulation in my childhood, loosely enforced, was to return home by dusk. In this environment, we were not just learning academically but also absorbing lessons in self-reliance.

The structured environment of a classroom, where formality and attentive listening were paramount, clashed with my innate wildness, a trait not uncommon in children but perhaps more pronounced in me. No child is born ready for the rigors of school; it's an adaptation, a gradual acclimatization to an environment vastly different from the unrestrained freedom of climbing trees and pretending to be Tarzan.

The end of that school year carried a leap forward in my awareness, much like a rite of passage in ancient cultures. I received my report card, a piece of paper that held little meaning to me until I handed it to Wayan, our gardener, who not only tended to the garden but also occasionally served as an interpreter of the adult world. After a moment of surprise, he said, "You didn't pass grade one."

This was a baffling concept to me.

"What does that mean?" I asked.

"It means you'll have to repeat the class."

I was dumbstruck. I literally reeled away from him, my head spinning. This struck a chord of frustration so deep that it drove me to stand on an outdoor table, shouting and weeping, a spectacle that remains etched in the memories of the local community.

This moment of youthful defiance was also a profound lesson in the consequences of failing to adapt to the expectations of a structured learning environment. It underscored a pivotal theme in my upbringing: the balance between the wild, natural instincts of my early years and the demands of a society structured around formal education and progression, a balance I was still learning to navigate.

Getaways to the Village

Each treasured excursion to Tianyar in the Karangasem regency, a village imbued with Bali's spiritual essence, felt like a holiday, a departure into a world where time resonated differently. With its rich traditions and cultural vibrancy, Tianyar provided a serene counterpoint to Legian's hustle.

Our visits to Tianyar several times a year, driven by the island's Hindu customs, were essential for participating in various ceremonies and cultural observances. These journeys were integral to our connection with Balinese heritage, marking special occasions or fulfilling spiritual duties.

The voyage to Tianyar began with an intricate circus act of fitting all five of us onto a single motorbike, a feat that demanded skill and balance. This initial leg of the journey was necessary to reach Denpasar's bus station, an hour away, where we would transition from the precarious motorbike to the relative safety and comfort of a bus. The winding and perilous roads to Tianyar made the bus our prudent choice for the latter part of our journey, despite our reluctance. Our dad, however, rode ahead on the motorbike.

Arriving at the bustling Denpasar bus station was an experience unto itself, an assault on the senses with mini-bus drivers vociferously announcing their destinations and fares, trying to attract passengers amidst the cacophony. The air was thick with the scents of market stalls selling an array of foods, mingling with less pleasant odors that invariably made our stomachs churn.

The bus, designed to seat merely eight passengers, was a menagerie on wheels, crammed with cages of chickens, goats, and pigs either alongside the human occupants or stacked precariously on the roof of the mini bus. The journey was far from comfortable, characterized by cramped quarters, a symphony of animal noises, smells of all kinds, and an omnipresent layer of grime.

My mother, Berate, harbored a particular aversion to car travel, which always induced motion sickness in her. Before each bus journey, she braced herself with seasickness pills, a common remedy among passengers unaccustomed to vehicle travel. Her experience with motorized transport was limited to motorbikes until her twenties, as they were the predominant mode of transportation over cars or buses in those years.

As we sat in the crowded mini-bus, I could feel every eye on me. New passengers climbed in, looking at me with intense curiosity.

"Whose boy is this?" they yelled, as if I were a statue that couldn't hear them.

"He is my son," my mother replied, her voice calm and matter-of-fact.

Their faces twisted with confusion, eyes darting between her dark features and my white skin. I couldn't help myself; I had to claim my place. I leaned forward and said, in fluent Balinese, "It's true. I'm her son, and I'm heading home just like you."

The bus went silent for a heartbeat before erupting into laughter and a thousand more questions. From that moment on, the ride became a theater fueled by their amazement.

Upon arrival, the minibus deposited us right at the doorstep of Berate's familial abode, located in the quaint seaside village. Situated in the shadow of the majestic Mount Agung, Tianyar was renowned for its influential priests and an air filled with mystical enchantments. It was where Berate's siblings and extended family continued to live and contribute to the spiritual and communal life, particularly around the village's central temple.

For me, Tianyar was a sanctuary, a second home where I felt an overwhelming sense of peace and welcome. Each visit was akin to a holiday, offering a new realm of freedom and exploration, where the village streets felt like they were exclusively mine to wander. Adjacent to Berate's family home was a *warung* that sold an assortment of goods, serving as the village's equivalent of a city shopping mall. Operated by a lineage of local families, the shop was a focal point of community interaction.

My dad always arrived before us with generous gifts of large sacks of rice and various culinary delights. These offerings, more than mere tradition, symbolized our respect and appreciation for the family. Whenever we visited Tianyar, even when seeing our own kin, we arrived bearing substantial gifts.

In this deeply rooted cultural exchange, the act of giving was reciprocal. The local families, despite their modest means, would respond with even grander gestures, providing us with meals. The significance of these meals cannot be understated. In a community where many struggled to provide for their own, the gift of food was a profound token of generosity. This was a crucial aspect of the local culture, reflecting a societal norm akin to a kingdom, a societal dance in which every host was expected to reciprocate with something greater than what they received. This tradition underscored the fundamental value of the Balinese culture of generosity and the deep respect shown through the act of giving and receiving.

In keeping with local tradition, the village elders often bestowed snacks and drinks upon us as welcoming gifts, a gesture of hospitality for those who had journeyed from afar. This practice emphasized the communal bond and respect for visitors, making each return to Tianyar a heartfelt reunion with a place and people that held a special place in my heart.

The family home in Tianyar was a nexus of familial and spiritual connection, inhabited by my mom's sister, her family, and a remarkable grandmother who, even at a hundred and five, was a paragon of vitality, living independently in a small adjoining unit. She was known affectionately as "Grandma" and her longevity and vigor were proof of the strength and wisdom of the villagers' way of life.

Tianyar was reputed to be a haven for some of the island's most spiritually adept individuals. These were people of profound energy and mysticism, capable of feats that, to the outside world, would seem like the stuff of legends.

Central to this spiritual tapestry was my uncle, a man whose deep spiritual prowess allowed him to navigate the realms of black and white magic. His role extended beyond the familial because he imparted his knowledge of Hinduism at the local school, bridging the sacred and the secular.

My fascination was always piqued in the special religious room where my uncle performed his spiritual rituals. Witnessing these acts was like stepping into a world that defied the conventional bounds of reality, leaving most Western minds in disbelief. These rituals weren't for public display, yet their impact was felt community-wide, serving a greater good.

To illustrate the extraordinary nature of his abilities, consider this: he could summon rain from a clear blue sky or dissipate storm clouds on the darkest days. These feats, though astounding to an outsider, were part of everyday life in Tianyar.

My curiosity about my uncle's mystical abilities never waned as I grew from a child into a teenager. The ease and swiftness with which he harnessed such profound power were both intriguing and awe-inspiring. Time and again, I would implore him to share his secrets, eager to understand and perhaps even wield such enigmatic forces myself. His response was always tempered with caution, emphasizing the immense responsibility that came with such power:

"It's not merely about having good intentions," he would say, "but about possessing the inner strength to contain and control such forces."

He promised that the day might come when he would pass on this profound knowledge to me, provided I matured into a person capable of handling its magnitude.

"The essence lies in the mantras," he revealed, hinting at the depth and complexity of the spiritual practices he mastered. But that day never arrived for me. As I grew older, I understood the complexities required of being such a person and it no longer interested me. His legacy continued, passing to a relative who would later play a pivotal role in my own life's ceremonies, intertwining the spiritual heritage of Tianyar into my personal journey.

Nyepi: A Day of Silence and Spectacle

> *The art of life isn't just found in constant motion, but also in the pauses that shape our perspective.*

In Bali, there's a day so profound that the entire island comes to a standstill. Once a year, during Nyepi, all normal activity ceases — no planes land or take off, the streets remain devoid of light, and even cooking is paused. Homes turn dark at night and become sanctuaries where no one steps outside, honoring a day dedicated to the spiritual realm, balancing our visible world with the unseen.

The night before Nyepi is anything but silent; it buzzes with anticipation and communal spirit. This is the evening when each community unveils massive, monstrous effigies made of bamboo and papier-mâché, crafted over several months by both children and adults. These creations, intended to be as fearsome as possible, are paraded through the streets to the rhythm of traditional music, their grotesque forms dancing atop bamboo stilts. Toward the end of the festive night, we loop back to our village and take the monsters to the beach, where we burn them in a symbolic ritual.

I always eagerly participated in these festivities, often as one of the carriers. In addition to bearing the weight of these towering figures, my role contributed to a performance, a dance of integration and community. As the only Westerner in the procession, I was strategically placed on the outer rim of the carrying stand. This placement wasn't just for balance; it was a statement that surprised and delighted onlookers, both locals and foreigners, bridging communities through a shared experience of awe and celebration.

Being a part of this, speaking fluent Balinese yet stumbling through English, I became a local curiosity, a symbol of cultural integration. Year after year, my involvement deepened my connections across villages, stretching far beyond Legian and solidifying my identity as a white boy who surprised many locals with the degree to which I had adapted to their culture.

Healing Through Nature

> *Sometimes, the most profound healing comes from the simplest elements of nature, teaching us that the answers we seek may already be within our grasp.*

I vividly recall a time when I fell gravely ill. No conventional medicine seemed to help and my condition only worsened. I was so weak that I had to be carried to the shower. The worry etched on my parents' faces deepened with each passing day, reflecting their growing concern over my mysterious ailment.

My Balinese mom asked her uncle, a revered spiritual master from Tianyar village, to help. He brought with him an assortment of what appeared to be simple bark and flowers. With meticulous care, he performed blessings on these natural elements, infusing them with an aura of sacredness. I was gently placed in a tub of water to which my mother added the blessed bark and flowers, immediately filling the air with a heavenly scent — a rich, intoxicating blend of floral and woody aromas that I found profoundly comforting and uplifting, even as a child. I remember that scent vividly; it seemed to transport me to a different dimension of tranquility.

I soaked there for an hour, letting the natural essence work its mysterious magic. By that afternoon, a remarkable transformation had occurred. My strength returned, allowing me to eat for the first time in days. By the next day, I felt revitalized, as though I had been reborn. The experience was a profound tribute to the healing power of nature and the ancient wisdom passed down through generations.

Was it truly the water, bark, and flowers that healed me, or was there something much grander at play? I may never know, but I now believe that I was healed by her uncle's blessings through nature. This incident deepened my belief in the unseen forces around us and the profound impact they can have on our lives. It was a vivid reminder that sometimes, the simplest elements of nature mixed with universal energy hold the most significant healing powers.

Italy for the Very First Time

> *Travel is the gateway to self-discovery, where each new landscape encountered paints another layer on the canvas of your identity.*

As I neared the age of nine, a new chapter unfolded with an invitation from my grandparents in Italy. They beckoned me to experience Italy for the first time, to immerse myself in the festive spirit of Christmas, and to relish the school holidays in December. Accompanied by Silvia, I embarked on the first flight of my young life, stepping into an adventure that promised new horizons and cherished memories.

Upon landing in Rome, I was thrust into a scene reminiscent of the movie *Cool Runnings*. The biting cold was a stark contrast to the warmth of Bali. My attire, lacking in layers, was hardly sufficient to fend off the chill. As I gazed out during our journey from the airport, my eyes widened at the sight of towering buildings, each one seeming to stretch higher than the last, a spectacle entirely alien to a boy who had never encountered such urban giants.

Silvia and I then made our way to her mother's residence in a grand apartment complex. Stepping into an elevator for the first time felt like venturing into a new realm — the sensation of being lifted was indescribable.

Once we reached the apartment, Silvia and her mother immediately sought assistance from their neighbors, hoping to find spare winter jackets for me, the boy from Bali unprepared for the cold.

Communication was a challenge. Silvia's mother and stepfather spoke no English and my grasp of their language was nonexistent. Silvia became our interpreter, bridging our worlds with her words. Her mother, driven by a nurturing instinct, was determined to feed me. She presented a succession of unfamiliar treats: fruits, then prosciutto, which, to my untrained eye, seemed like raw meat; and finally, Nutella spread on bread, a universal delight for children, followed by a refreshing juice in a box, a novelty for me, hailing as I did from a place where such conveniences were yet to arrive. Each offering was a new taste adventure, a warm gesture of welcome in a foreign land.

The arrival day was a revelation in every sense. Dinner introduced a new ritual; gathering around an elegantly set table adorned with a pristine white cloth and an inviting array of breads. Then came the pasta, a dish that quickly won my heart. Dipping bread into olive oil was a delightful experience; the oil's rich flavor was unlike anything I had encountered back home in Bali, igniting my curiosity about this new culinary world.

The surroundings added to my awe: the home's cleanliness, ornate decor, spacious rooms, and luxuriously smooth bedsheets was a display of opulence I had never seen before. Amidst these luxuries, Silvia's mother stood out — a figure of authority and warmth, her regal bearing matched by the kindness of her smile, making me feel both out of place and warmly embraced in this unfamiliar, grand setting.

The day following our arrival was a whirlwind of introductions and generosity. News of my presence quickly spread throughout the apartment complex, drawing in neighbors eager to meet the new visitor from Bali. They brought gifts of clothing, an act of kindness for which I was immensely thankful. My shyness was overshadowed by my gratitude, especially since I had arrived ill-equipped for the winter chill. This communal warmth and the swift embrace from Silvia's neighbors offered a comforting welcome to a place so far from home.

Silvia and I went for a walk around the neighborhood, the bustling streets of Rome offered an eye-opening exploration, distinctly different from anything I had experienced before. This whirlwind of new sights and sounds was just the beginning.

During our walk, Silvia mentioned that my grandparents were coming that day to pick me up and take me several hours away to their home, where I would spend some time with them.

Later that afternoon, my grandparents — people I barely knew at the time, arrived at Silvia's home. It marked the first occasion I would be alone with them, and the start of something unfamiliar.

Although we had met several times before, this greeting was more memorable. My grandma spoke English and my grandfather spoke no English, and I, lacking both English and Italian, felt the silence between us. Yet, he was determined to claim his place in my mind. He began to speak with a frantic, rhythmic energy — a flurry of melodic vowels and sharp consonants — using a beautiful shorthand of gestures to bridge the silence between us.

He was reaching for a memory, desperate to ensure I knew exactly who he was to me. With his eyes locked on mine, he began to pantomime a story: his hands flew through the air, tracing the arc of an object, and then he tapped his weathered index finger sharply against his forehead. He was reenacting the infamous afternoon I had launched a battery at him.

He held a look of mock gravity, his brows furrowed in a stern, theatrical pout as if he were still nursing the phantom bruise from years ago. For a heartbeat, the room went still as I searched his face. Then, the sternness evaporated. His eyes crinkled into a map of fine lines, and we both dissolved into a messy, breathless laughter. In that moment, the battery wasn't just a story about a mischievous child; it was the bridge that brought us together, proving that love doesn't always need a translator.

My young mind struggled with the foreign sounds of my grandmother's name, "Daniela", leading me to affectionately dub her "Dadong," an Indonesian term for grandma. My grandfather became "Mr. P" - endearing names that would last into my adulthood.

As we mingled and tried to get to know one another, a sudden comment cut through the moment: *"It's time to go, Luca."*

My mind raced. Panic rose inside me. I couldn't face leaving Silvia, stepping once again into the unknown without her and going with people I barely knew.

The panic took over, and I ran, disappearing into the freezing corners of Rome while the neighborhood began to search for me. I was terrified of being forced into a home with people who still felt like strangers to me, so I crouched behind a steel dumpster, fighting a war with my own mind.

How long can I stay here? I wondered. It's freezing. Should I wait until they drive away? If I go back now after making such a scene, how will they look at me?"

I was stuck between the biting cold and the fear of what came next. The incident turned into quite the spectacle until Silvia found me hours later, her sooth-ing reassurances calming my fears. She promised it would only be a matter of days before she returned for me, a pledge that eventually coaxed me from my hiding spot, ready to embark on another chapter of this Italian journey.

Before I knew it, I found myself in a car that oozed luxury, heading toward my birth mother's home, nestled in the picturesque village of Valdagno. The drive was enchanting, with winding roads that climbed a hill, offering a panoramic view of the sprawling village below. The entrance to my grand-parents' home featured an automatic gate, a marvel to my unaccustomed eyes, deepening my sense of won-der and intrigue.

The property unfolded like a scene from a story-book, with another gate rolling open as we descended beneath the house to park. This world of automation was enthralling, much different from my familiar sur-roundings in Bali. Just below the living quarters, I dis-covered rooms that captured my imagination: one housed a billiards table, while another was a haven of mechanical wonders, filled with RC airplanes and an assortment of tools and machines. These spaces in-stantly drew me in, combining two of my passions and offering a sanctuary that felt both exciting and overwhelming. Before even setting foot in the main living area, I was already enamored with this new environment, feeling a mix of awe and a curious sense of smallness in such an expansive world.

The house lacked the creaks and groans I was used to from the wooden floors and doors back home. The space was immaculate, a striking embodiment of perfection and opulence; a dwelling fit for royalty.

Every corner of the house was thoughtfully designed, providing a place for everything, a stark contrast to the modest dimensions of my familiar three-by-three-meter space in Bali. My grandmother, Dadong, took me on a tour of the house, eventually leading me to the room where I would be sleeping. It contained two single beds, preserved in time, belonging to Marta and her sister Anna. The room had retained its original state from their childhood to their transition into adulthood, enveloping me in a tangible sense of history and connection to my roots.

Dadong's foresight in learning English was aimed at facilitating our future conversations. Despite her efforts, my linguistic repertoire was limited to the basic English I had picked up on the bustling streets of Legian, far from sufficient for any meaningful exchanges. Our communication often devolved into a dance of nods and gestures, a silent language of understanding that bridged the gap between our worlds. While she embraced the challenge of learning a new language in the latter years of her life, Grandpa remained rooted in his traditional ways, embodying an old-school ethos that eschewed the need for such adaptations. This dynamic created a unique blend of interactions, where unspoken understanding was often louder than words, illustrating a profound familial bond that transcended language barriers.

During those early days with Dadong, our time together followed a comforting routine. Each morning, I would find her in the kitchen, where breakfast awaited me — a familiar sight of Nutella spread on white bread alongside a glass of milk, all meticulously prepared on the dining table. After breakfast, while I immersed myself in television, Dadong would tidy and clean until her chores were concluded around 10 a.m. Then it was our time. She would bring out games, crafting moments of connection despite our language barrier.

Those initial days were about adjustment, acclimating to a new rhythm and space that felt worlds apart from Bali. As the days unfolded, though, a sense of disorientation began to creep in. The novelty of my surroundings morphed into a haze of confusion. Without the ability to communicate verbally, I felt adrift, caught in a limbo of waiting and wondering, uncertain of when Silvia would return or when I would see Bali again. It was a profound isolation, where the expansiveness of time and the confines of space mingled, leaving me to navigate my thoughts and uncertainties in silent contemplation.

During a morning outing, we ventured into town, with our first stop at a florist's shop. Curious, I asked, "Why are we here?"

She replied, "We're picking flowers for your mother."

This statement left me bewildered. In my young mind, my mother was in Bali. At seven, my world revolved around my Balinese family, whom I considered my true parents. The idea that they might not be my birth parents had not yet dawned on me, and this new revelation stirred a mix of confusion and curiosity within me.

At a nearby cemetery, we walked along the solemn paths to a wall inscribed with names, the final resting places of our ancestors. Dadong gently explained, "These names represent our relatives who rest here."

Puzzled, I asked, "But where exactly?" pointing to the wall. She clarified that beneath our feet lay the buried, a concept that bewildered my young mind because I had never attended a burial. Observing her tears, I found myself engulfed in a maelstrom of confusion, grappling with the stark reality of mortality and familial bonds, a poignant moment etched in my memory.

We then ventured into the heart of town, where the bustling central district awaited. Dadong skillfully maneuvered her car into a parking spot that required payment, a process that intrigued me, given my unfamiliarity with such organized urban landscapes. We embarked on a leisurely stroll through quaint lanes, each flanked by tall, uniquely designed houses, their distinctiveness capturing my curiosity.

Our journey unfolded through a series of visits to specialized shops, another novel experience for me. First, we entered a bakery where the aroma of fresh bread wafted through the air and Dadong selected the finest loaves of the day. Next, we visited a butcher's shop where she carefully chose quality meats. In each shop, Dadong was greeted warmly, a familiar presence, echoing the sense of community I sensed in Bali, yet in a markedly different setting.

The concept of shopping from one shop to another for specific items was foreign to me because I was accustomed to the markets back home where everything was available in one place. The day concluded with a trip to a grocery store, a setting I found more familiar, yet I couldn't help but wonder about the efficiency of our earlier errands. This peculiar shopping routine left me with a multitude of questions, but I could not hope to satisfy my curiosity due to the language barrier.

With each new day, my sense of disorientation deepened. Silvia's promise to return after a few days lingered in my mind, yet a week had elapsed with no sign of her. An overwhelming desire to escape back to Bali gnawed at me as I navigated through a whirlwind of unfamiliar experiences and faces. Dadong frequently escorted me to the homes of her acquaintances, an endeavor that initially filled me with reluctance. The sight of unfamiliar faces and unknown environments made me hesitant to leave the sanctuary of the car.

However, my curiosity was often piqued by the sight of their offerings, an array of uniquely wrapped Italian desserts, both intriguing and inviting. These were the very treats I had glimpsed during our shopping excursions, their allure now coaxing me into the homes of Dadong's friends. Despite my initial shyness, the prospect of discovering the flavors hidden within those special wrappings gradually drew me out, enticing me to venture into new surroundings, one sweet treat at a time.

The arrival of a new day brought an unexpected gift; the discovery of a friend, someone with whom I shared a close blood tie, but whose significance in my life I had yet to fully grasp. This newfound companionship emerged during a visit to my aunt Anna's house. The concepts of aunts and uncles were still abstract notions to me then, their roles and relationships not entirely understood.

In the heart of my aunt's home was Ema, my cousin, whose birth preceded mine by just five days. Like my grandparents, our connection transcended the need for words; we communicated through gestures, nods, and shared laughter, finding common ground despite the language barrier. There were also my other younger cousins, Annie and Eli. My uncle whom I met later, newly married and yet to start his own family, was another figure in this new chapter of my life.

During a visit to the mountains, an entirely new experience unfolded before me. Dressed in thick, brightly colored gear, I felt like a character from a Power Rangers episode. The vivid suits seemed out of place against the natural backdrop of the snow-covered slopes.

Ema took on the role of guide and companion, leading me up a steep hill with a bobsled in tow, secured by a simple piece of rope. At the summit, he motioned for me to sit at the front of the sled, and before I could fully grasp the situation, we were hurtling down the slope. The exhilaration of that first descent ignited a spark within me, fueling a desire to ascend and descend repeatedly, each time with the same enthusiasm.

Amid these moments of thrill and excitement was a simple yet profoundly memorable experience — enjoying my grandmother's ham and cheese sandwich during a brief lunch break. That sandwich was a culinary revelation, introducing my palate to flavors that were both comforting and novel. The memory of that taste, intertwined with the crisp mountain air and the joy of the day's adventures, is still vivid in my memory.

When Christmas arrived, I was introduced to a tradition that was entirely foreign to me. I naively assumed it was someone's birthday celebration. My grandmother's introduction to the holiday involved a tree adorned with gifts, a practice attributed to a mysterious figure named Santa Claus, whose identity was as perplexing to me as the tradition itself.

On Christmas morning, with excitement in the air, my grandmother ushered me to the tree, which was brimming with wrapped presents. The sight was bewildering, totally incomparable to anything I had experienced before. She handed me a large, festively wrapped package. Still grappling with the customs of this new culture, I unwrapped it to discover a toy car set. This wasn't just any toy; it was a circuit track with cars that raced at the push of a button, a novel concept for a child accustomed to simpler playthings.

The ensuing days were a blur of new experiences: playing endlessly with the toy car track, getting lost in cartoons and movies on the VHS player, and accompanying my grandmother on drives. This Christmas marked a profound moment in my life, a first brush with European traditions for a boy from Bali who, despite his white skin, spoke only Balinese and was just beginning to grasp the notion that the people surrounding him were his family, connected by blood and history.

VHS-C recordings

Some years later, during another trip to Italy, my Italian grandparents showed me VHS-C recordings, a series of videos they had made to meticulously document their multiple visits to Bali. These recordings serve as a precious window into my past, an invaluable archive that traces the contours of my early childhood. Laden with moments both mundane and monumental, these tapes offer me a unique view of the world into which I was born, a world my young self was too small to remember, but one I can now see through the lens of hindsight.

Among these visual treasures, the snippets featuring Marta, my mother, are particularly poignant. Though brief, each appearance she makes on screen is a revelation, a fleeting glimpse into her essence and the vibrancy of her spirit. These recordings go beyond typical familial documentation; they encapsulate the entire spectrum of our life in Bali — the jubilant celebrations, intimate birthdays, and culturally rich ceremonies — painting a vivid picture of the dynamic backdrop against which our lives unfolded.

This archival footage, bequeathed to me by the thoughtful foresight of my grandparents, serves as a bridge to my past, offering concrete imagery to the stories and anecdotes I've heard over the years, and grounding them in reality. Through these recordings, I've been granted the opportunity to witness first-hand the environment, the people, and the myriad events that shaped my early years. They provide a deeper understanding of my roots and the cultural tapestry that is my heritage, helping me piece together the narrative of who I was then and who I have become.

Among the visual chronicles captured in these recordings is a vivid portrayal of John's home, a place synonymous with celebration and communal joy. John had a tradition of hosting grand parties, particularly for birthdays, a gesture of his generosity and love for bringing people together. These gatherings manifested John's deep appreciation for Balinese culture and music, epitomized by his annual inclusion of the *jegog* performance.

The *jegog,* a grand ensemble of bamboo xylophones, stands as a cultural icon within these recordings. Each instrument, crafted from bamboo tubes of varying lengths and sizes, contributes to a symphony that is as visually striking as it is aurally captivating. The rhythms are compelling, a cascade of energetic beats and intricate melodies that invite not just listening but total immersion. Accompanying the *jegog's* powerful sonority are traditional Balinese dancers, whose movements add a layer of storytelling to the music, creating a captivating performance.

The scale of these musical celebrations was such that transporting the *jegog* required not one but two trucks: one for the substantial instruments and another for the ensemble of musicians and dancers who brought them to life. Through these recordings, the essence of John's home as a hub of cultural celebration and personal milestones is vividly preserved, offering a glimpse into the joyous interplay of music, dance, and communal harmony that defined our familial and social gatherings.

One of the recordings, capturing the vibrant celebration of my fourth birthday, holds a special place in my heart. The video reveals John's garden transformed into a bustling epicenter of festivity, teeming with his expatriate friends and their children, who, like him, had woven their lives into the fabric of the island. This gathering was a communal event, a microcosm of the diverse community we were part of where local families mingled with newcomers, all drawn together by the enchanting rhythms of the *jegog*.

The camera pans across the garden, now a sea of friendly faces and laughter, capturing a moment of pure childhood delight as I, the birthday boy, delve into the ritual of gift-opening. The focal point of this joyous occasion was a large plastic toy push car, a novel marvel for us island kids. The video shows me surrounded by a cohort of local friends, excitedly navigating the toy car through the garden's dirt paths.

This scene, preserved in the grainy authenticity of the VHS-C recording, showcases a place where cultural lines blurred, and where children played in unison, united by the simple joy of a new toy and the shared experience of music and celebration. Watching this video years later, I'm reminded of the warmth and inclusivity that marked my early years, a time when joy was found in the simplest of pleasures and community was as much a part of our lives as family.

Our childhood was steeped in simplicity and ingenuity, where the art of toy-making was passed down through the community. We found joy in the aforementioned kites we crafted from plastic bags, melding the material to bamboo frames with the careful application of incense heat, a ritual overseen by the guiding hands of the adults around us. This was our entertainment, made possible by our own resourcefulness and connection to the environment. Because of this simplicity, the arrival of a plastic toy car was a symbol of luxury, a gateway to new realms of imagination that were previously uncharted in our island play.

The notion of "luxury" took on a new dimension and my world was greatly expanded when my Italian grandparents, eager to blend their heritage with our Balinese upbringing, introduced me and my Balinese brothers to Timezone in Kuta, a place as foreign to us as the concept of winter in tropical Bali. Our adventures had previously been confined to the natural landscapes of Tianyar village, making Timezone an overwhelming sensory experience.

The escalator, a moving staircase that led to this wonderland of games and lights, was an obstacle in itself, introducing me to modernity with a mix of awe and apprehension. The gentle coaxing of the reassuring adults and the calming presence of my grandparents and Balinese brothers were necessary to bridge my trust between familiar ground and the undulating steps of this mechanical marvel. This introduction to the dazzling allure of arcade games was a pivotal moment in my childhood, expanding my understanding of play and intertwining my cultural roots with new, exciting experiences of joy and discovery.

Inside Timezone, amidst the cacophony of sounds and the kaleidoscope of lights, the arcade games stood as alien contraptions to my unacquainted eyes. My brothers and I, guided by our grandmother's attempts to explain, navigated this new terrain with a mix of curiosity and confusion. The games somehow missed their mark with me, leaving me more bewildered than enchanted.

In this landscape of electronic amusements, the pony ride — a feature that should have delighted a child — loomed as yet another challenge, its unfamiliarity breeding a sense of unease rather than excitement. Finding solace in the predictable motion of the escalator that led to Timezone, I chose to spend hours riding up and down with my grandmother, transforming the moving staircase into my personal amusement ride. I was a child literally stuck between two worlds, finding comfort in the gentle ebb and flow of a mechanical marvel.

The day's journey of new experiences didn't end with the escalator rides. Adjacent to Timezone, located in the bustling heart of Kuta, was a McDonald's, a place as foreign to me as the arcade had been. My grandparents, eager to introduce me to another facet of Western culture, presented me with my first-ever burger from this iconic fast-food chain. The anticipation of this novel culinary experience quickly turned to dismay as the unfamiliar flavors clashed with my palate, culminating in an immediate and visceral rejection. My first repulsive encounter with a McDonald's burger lives forever in my memory, and it shaped my culinary preferences in a way that would endure over the years.

The experiences of that day underscore a profound truth: our most vivid memories and preferences are often forged in the simplest of moments, through experiences that challenge or comfort us. The joy I found in the rhythmic ride of the escalator, juxtaposed with the jarring introduction to fast food, serves as a reminder that delight and contentment are not always found in grandiose or novel experiences, but can stem from the most basic and familiar comforts.

CHAPTER III

In the Space Between Two Worlds

Life often places us at the intersection of two or more worlds, each offering its own lessons, challenges, and opportunities for growth. Whether we find ourselves between cultures, environments, or different phases of life, these in-between spaces can be some of the most transformative experiences we encounter. While it may feel disorienting at times, living between different worlds grants us a broader perspective, a richer understanding of life's complexities, and a deeper capacity for growth.

Navigating multiple worlds is more than just a geographical or cultural shift; it's an ongoing journey of adapting, reflecting, and learning. When we find ourselves in unfamiliar places or situations, we are forced to confront what we've always known and measure it against what we're discovering. This process helps us develop resilience and adaptability as we learn to navigate the unknown while holding onto what remains important. It also expands our capacity for empathy and understanding as we encounter people and traditions that challenge our preconceived notions.

The beauty of living between two worlds is that it teaches us flexibility, not just in how we approach external changes, but in how we respond internally. We learn to hold space for multiple perspectives and begin to see that there isn't always one "right" way to approach life. This flexibility allows us to adapt without losing ourselves, and to evolve while remaining true to the core of who we are. Over time, the ability to move between different worlds becomes one of our greatest strengths, empowering us to thrive in diverse environments and connect with people from all walks of life.

However, the experience of navigating two worlds is not without its challenges. It can often feel like being pulled in opposite directions, where one world asks us to hold onto tradition while another encourages us to embrace change. In these moments, we may feel a sense of conflict, torn between the familiar comfort of what we've always known and the excitement of stepping into the unknown. However, this tension is where growth occurs. It's where we learn to blend the wisdom of the past with the possibilities of the future.

Living between worlds allows us to become bridges, not just for ourselves but for others. We develop a skill for finding common ground between seemingly opposing perspectives, learning to integrate different influences in ways that create harmony. This ability to bridge gaps — whether between cultures, people, or ideas — gives us a unique strength: the capacity to foster connection in places where division might otherwise prevail. It enables us to carry forward the richness of each world we've inhabited, building something new from the diverse experiences we've encountered.

It's most important to remember that life is not a straight path. Each world we enter and each transition we face adds another thread to the tapestry of our experience. While it may sometimes feel like we don't fully belong in any one place, the truth is that every world we touch becomes part of us. We are not defined by a single culture, location, or experience, but by the ways we weave these influences together.

The key is to embrace the fluidity of life, welcoming the lessons that come with stepping into new worlds while cherishing the foundations that shaped us. It's about finding comfort in the unknown and realizing that with each new experience, we become more whole, more aware, and more resilient. Living between worlds teaches us that our growth is limitless, shaped by every experience, challenge, and connection we make along the way.

As we continue on this journey, let us remember that the richness of life comes from its diversity. Every world we inhabit — whether it's a place, a community, or a phase of life — offers something unique. By embracing both the familiar and the unknown, we open ourselves to the endless possibilities that life has to offer. This journey between worlds is not just about adaptation, it's about growth, reflection, and discovering the beauty that comes from living in the spaces in between.

Going to International School

As I mentioned, John's perspective on education, shaped by his upbringing, was not entirely supportive of traditional schooling. However, recognizing the crucial role of English in my future, he made a decisive intervention. Despite our unconventional relationship, and my upbringing with Berate and her family, John was more a figure in my life than a traditional father. His presence and decisions were becoming increasingly significant. His candid, almost jesting warning about "selling Coca Cola on the beach" if I didn't learn English was his way of emphasizing the importance of language skills in my life.

At nearly seven years old, following my first-grade setback, John's determination that I learn English marked a significant transition. It was a practical decision, reflecting his understanding that, regardless of his personal views on education, acquiring English was essential for my future. This pivotal moment was about opening doors to new possibilities and broader horizons.

Within just a week of stressing the necessity of learning English, John shared the exciting news: he was sending me to an international school. The year

1998 marked the beginning of this new chapter at one of the two international schools available in Bali at that time, SIS (Sanur Independent School). The other was BIS (Bali International School). Both schools were located in Sanur, about an hour away from where we lived in Legian. My half-sister, Ziska, who was two and a half years my senior, was already attending SIS. Every morning, my mother, Berate, would walk me to Ziska's house so we could board the school bus together.

The bus ride became a daily ritual that connected me to the sounds of a new world. On the bus, amidst a chorus of voices, children sang along to the latest hits playing on the radio. While they effortlessly joined in, I struggled to decipher the lyrics. Western music was a novel concept to me, a world apart from the ceremonial tunes of local music.

Day after day, as the same songs echoed through the bus, my ears began to tune into the rhythm and language of this foreign music. My understanding of English improved with each passing day, not just in comprehension but also in my ability to distinguish between different genres and expressions within the songs. I started recognizing the nuances that defined masculine and feminine songs - distinctions that simply do not exist in Balinese music.

Embarking on my journey at the international school felt like stepping into an entirely new realm. For the first time, I was surrounded by peers who looked like me, with white skin and blonde hair, the polar opposite of the community I was accustomed to. This environment awakened my awareness of my own physical similarity to these children, yet I felt a profound disconnect due to the language barrier. Despite our similar appearances, I experienced an unexpected sense of alienation because my heart and identity remained deeply rooted in Balinese culture. I was a Balinese boy at my core, yet here I was, among peers to whom I should ostensibly relate, grappling with a sense of belonging, and struggling to bridge two worlds within me.

In the nurturing environment of my new school, I quickly formed meaningful friendships, but one particular friend, Tiziano, a Swiss-French boy, stood out. His warmth and kindness made him feel more like a brother than just a friend. Over time, Tiziano introduced me to the intriguing world of interacting with girls, sparking new and exciting conversations during our break times. Our camaraderie was put to the test when Gala, a new student of Spanish descent and arguably the most charming girl at school, arrived. Tiziano and I found ourselves in a friendly rivalry, each hoping to win her affection - our first foray into schoolboy crushes.

Amidst this new social landscape, Tiziano became my linguistic bridge, blending Indonesian with English to aid my understanding. While my English was still developing and far from perfect, this allowed me to communicate and build connections. The school was a melting pot of languages, with many students fluent in Indonesian, while others, new to the country, were just beginning to learn. This diverse linguistic environment fostered a unique sense of community among us. Despite our different backgrounds, we found common ground and learned to understand each other.

The international school presented a dramatic difference to my Balinese school experience, featuring a varied curriculum that required us to move between different classrooms for various subjects throughout the day. The canteen, while a familiar concept, differed significantly in terms of pricing. Unlike the affordable options at my previous school, the snacks here were pricier and the money my mom gave me often fell short for canteen purchases. There were days when my bag lacked pre-packed snacks or lunch and my pocket money was insufficient.

When I needed it, Ziska became my savior, kindly buying me snacks from a small *warung* located just opposite the school. These after-school treats, modest yet heartfelt, often served as the highlight of my day, providing a small taste of comfort amid the new and unfamiliar environment of the international school.

On my very first day, with no proficiency in English, I was fortunate to be placed under the tutelage of Miss Pam. She was an extraordinary educator, skilled in teaching English to students like me who came from non-English-speaking backgrounds. Her expertise and guidance were instrumental in my swift progress as I began to articulate English words, grasp the basics of writing, and learn the alphabet.

Gradually, I progressed from recognizing letters to forming words and eventually constructing complete sentences — the humble beginnings of my journey with the English language.

Mr. John, the arts teacher, became another pivotal figure in my academic life. He welcomed me into the realm of arts, a domain where I discovered my innate talent and newfound passion. Mr. John's gentle demeanor and caring approach resonated deeply with me, creating a connection that was both educational and soulful. His influence extended beyond the classroom, imparting lessons and insights that I still cherish and apply to this day.

Under his guidance, I learned the importance of internalizing knowledge, an approach that mirrored the teachings I had absorbed in my Balinese upbringing. Both in Bali and at this international school, I was surrounded by educators who taught from the heart, prioritizing empathy and understanding over ego.

Didi's and Ziska's home became a sanctuary for me, serving as my third home. After school, as the bus dropped us off at Ziska's place, I would spend my afternoons there until evening approached. Didi, with her ever-open heart, not only provided a warm environment but also took an active role in my education, assisting me with homework and mentoring me in English after her workday ended. She diligently worked on teaching me the alphabet and the correct pronunciation of English words.

Recognizing the need for more structured language support, Didi enlisted the help of her friend Rita, an Indonesian woman proficient in English. Rita's ability to translate and explain concepts from Indonesian to English was a blessing. She visited a couple of times a week, providing tailored tutoring sessions that significantly enhanced my language skills. Her guidance was invaluable, bridging the gap between my Balinese upbringing and the new English-speaking world I was navigating.

Didi's home was a hub of vibrant interactions and learning, blending the comfort of familiar local playmates with the novelty of school friends, which aided my burgeoning English skills. It was also a lively playground where she engaged us in a variety of enchanting games and introduced us to snacks and candies from Australia, a far cry from what was available in Bali.

Mbak Sur, the housekeeper, often prepared delightful Indonesian instant noodles or fresh fruit bowls for us, providing a comforting treat after a day at school. This duality of environments — my Balinese roots and Didi's home — offered me a unique glimpse into Western family life. I began to grasp the nuances of Western culture, from the diverse foods, to interacting with peers who looked like me but seemed to come from a different world.

The afternoons I spent at Ziska's, mingling with her friends and immersing myself in their camaraderie often sparked a desire in me to extend those warm moments into sleepovers. Occasionally, as the evening drew close and my mother hadn't arrived from her work at John's, Didi would gently remind me, "Luca, time to go home." Despite understanding the practicality of her words, a part of me wrestled with a sense of dislocation, questioning why I needed to leave a place that felt so much like home.

There were instances when my mother, Berate, would suggest, "Why don't you sleep at Didi's?" upon my late arrival home. Although I knew this option was available, I felt rejected by my Balinese mother every time she suggested it, and very lost, as if I didn't belong in her home. These feelings, however fleeting, left a significant imprint on my young heart.

The duality of where home truly was, whether at Didi's warm abode or with my mother just a short walk away, painted a complex picture of belonging and identity during my formative years.

While John was engrossed in his own world, his sporadic appearances to pick me up from school in his sporty car were memorable yet puzzling experiences. I still viewed him as a distant tourist, and these rare moments of interaction left me perplexed, unable to fully grasp why this occasional visitor was involved in my daily routine, ferrying me to the very home where my mom dedicated her days to work. This duality of life experiences enriched my understanding of the different worlds I straddled.

Leaving Legian

With Bali's growing popularity and the transformation of land into hotels in the early 2000s, John faced a dilemma. His cherished bamboo house in Legian, built on leased land, was nearing the end of its lease.

Skyrocketing land prices made it impossible for John to extend the lease, especially after he had invested all his funds into building Paul Michael's estate, a project that Paul himself had never formally settled. As I've been told, agreements of that scale were often sealed with a handshake back then, especially between close friends like John and Paul. With no other option, John decided to relocate. Pak Nyoman offered John his land near the quaint village of Klepekan, about forty minutes inland from Legian. Known for its skilled craftsmen, Klepekan was also home to John's manufacturing base. This offer allowed John to build two homes in exchange for long-term rent on the land, all arranged under a handshake, which would prove to be a mistake I will explain in a later chapter.

Another hurdle presented itself: John didn't have sufficient funds to construct his new home on this land. Fortunately, Silvia stepped in, securing the necessary finances. With the clock ticking on the lease in Legian, they managed to complete two Toraja houses, a design from South Sulawesi in Klepekan, just in time.

I was only nine years old when I started spending more time there with John and Silvia, beginning my gradual adaptation to life with them. As my English improved, I began to communicate more effectively, slowly piecing together their roles in my life, although it remained somewhat hazy.

Accustomed to living in various environments, the concept of staying in one place felt foreign to me. There were days when my mom would instruct me to sleep over at John and Silvia's, locking the gates after she left to prevent me from leaving. This left me feeling trapped and confused about why I couldn't go home. Despite repeated explanations that John was my father and Silvia my stepmother, I had not yet fully grasped the nature of these relationships.

The afternoons were a time of solitude and confusion for me after my mom left. Neither John nor Silvia engaged much in play or interaction, leaving me bored and alone in the kitchen until they came in for dinner. The concept of a family gathering around the table for an evening meal, as most Western families do, was absent in this new setting. I often found myself alone in the kitchen, wrestling with a sense of disorientation as day turned into evening.

My mom usually cooked dinner and ensured I was fed before her shift ended, but in those early days, she stayed late to comfort me through the transition, which I didn't fully understand at the time.

After John and Silvia moved to Klepekan, my Balinese dad had begun working as a gardener. I sometimes heard him whisper to my mom, "Let's go. It's getting dark," and when she hesitated, he'd get upset. Still, there were moments when I felt more love and care from both of them than from my father or Silvia. It was a strange, unfamiliar feeling - something I didn't know how to accept or make sense of.

Bedtime brought its own peculiar routine in this new living arrangement, which felt like a sleepover. I crafted a makeshift bed on the floor using two large pillows, positioning myself across from John and Silvia's bed.

Pak Nyoman's residence, merely a hundred meters away, quickly became a sanctuary for me, almost like a second home. He had known me all my life, establishing a fatherly bond that made my presence in his home feel natural. Daily, I found myself gravitating toward his welcoming household, adhering to Balinese customs by addressing him and his wife as "dad" and "mom" - a mark of respect ingrained in me from an early age.

Their home was a haven of openness and warmth where I was embraced as one of their own. They had two boys, Koming and Kadek, who were several years older and whom I looked upon as my older brothers. I often spent my nights there, sleeping with Nyoman and his wife, and I preferred the comfort of their proper mattress to the makeshift bed of pillows at John's. The stability and familiarity of Pak Nyoman's brick house, free from eerie night sounds, also provided a sense of security and normalcy that I sorely needed at the time.

In the embrace of Pak Nyoman's family, I found myself enveloped in the local traditions and ceremonies; a unique white boy in the village, fluent in Balinese yet distinct in appearance. The evenings were special for me, not just for the delectable meals prepared by Pak Nyoman's wife but also for the adventures that awaited at his favorite *warung*. He indulged me, allowing me to navigate the short stretch of road on his motorbike, a thrilling privilege. At the *warung,* I was treated like royalty, free to choose whatever my heart desired.

I immersed myself in village life, engaging naturally with the local children. They introduced me to a variety of village activities, such as crafting *ogoh-ogoh* monsters from mud that we harvested from the small river and transformed into malleable clay. We would then paint and dress our monsters with bits and pieces we found at home and parade them through the streets in the dark afternoon. We ventured into the rice fields to catch eels, a skill that was both new and thrilling to me. The surrounding rice paddies weren't just agricultural land; they were our playground, where we flew massive kites, navigating the slender paths between fields with the strings taut in our hands. Each day was a lesson in the simple yet enriching village traditions, connecting me even more deeply with the land and its lively culture.

My first profound spiritual experience occurred around the age of nine. On a radiant day, while heading to the local *warung,* I encountered a familiar villager with a notably large fishing rod. My curiosity piqued, I inquired about his fishing spot, having only known small-scale fishing in rice fields until then. He replied, "I'm off to the river temple to try out my new rod. I've never fished there before. Would you like to join me?"

I had never heard of this place but I felt compelled to follow him. We ventured down a narrow, previously unnoticed path just a stone's throw from my usual haunt at the local *warung*. The pathway, shrouded in a canopy of trees, gradually dimmed our surroundings, creating a mystical ambiance. Eventually, it opened up to reveal a temple of unparalleled beauty beside a gently flowing river. It was my first encounter with such a serene and picturesque setting, much grander than the rice field fishing of my past. This experience was one of many that connected me to the deeper, spiritual essence of village life.

He meticulously set up the rod, baited it, and cast it into the river.

"Luca, hold the rod. I'm going to sit in the *bale*," he said, referring to a small resting hut.

Minutes passed when, unexpectedly, it began to rain despite the clear blue sky. Such brief showers under sunny skies weren't unusual so I stayed put, anticipating a fish's tug. However, the rain intensified, compelling me to withdraw the rod and seek refuge in the *bale*. Remarkably, the moment I reached the shelter, the rain ceased.

With undiminished optimism, we ventured back to the river under the still sunny and cloudless sky and cast the rod again. Like a precise replay, raindrops began to fall as soon as the bait touched the water. We retreated once more, hoping it was just a fleeting shower. After a patient wait, we tried again, only to be greeted by rain yet again! It was then that the elderly man had an epiphany — the temple was signaling that our intrusion was not welcome. With a respectful acknowledgment of the temple's silent message, we packed up and left the sacred space.

As we exited the temple's vicinity, a peculiar observation struck me: the ground outside the temple's boundary was bone dry, while within it was damp, a clear demarcation that the rain was confined to the temple's sacred precincts. It was a moment that intertwined nature, spirituality, and local beliefs, undeniably demonstrating the village's mystical aura.

This personal experience of the spiritual beliefs and practices of my upbringing illuminated the reasons behind those traditions — why we kept lights on through the night and why playtime ended at 6 p.m. I understood that these weren't mere superstitions but acknowledgments of a deeper spiritual rhythm that dictated a respectful coexistence between humans and unseen realms.

This was a call to heed the age-old wisdom of our ancestors, to recognize the signs and signals from the spiritual realm, and to live in harmony with them.

Reflecting on my childhood, I realized that my fears could have been mitigated by adhering to these cultural teachings and understanding the balance and boundaries set by our forebears to navigate the interplay between our world and the one that lies beyond our ordinary perception.

As I settled more into life with John and Silvia, I began to perceive the nuances of John's personality, discovering facets of him that resonated with me despite our limited interactions. He often secluded himself in his room, creating an invisible barrier that I, in my timidity, seldom crossed. Silvia, too, remained somewhat distant during the day, leaving me to navigate this new living environment largely on my own.

The financial strain of building a second home necessitated a major change in my life; a switch to a more affordable school. Thus, I was introduced to Sunrise School. Nestled amidst the familiar backdrop of lush rice fields, the school offered an educational experience vastly different from that of SIS. Its proximity to our home in Klepekan and its distinctive pedagogical approach promised a new chapter in my learning, once more in tune with the environment and community I was growing to love.

At Sunrise School, I found myself immersed in an atmosphere that blended academic learning with the natural world around us, vastly different from the more conventional environment I had known at SIS. The setting echoed the familiar rhythms of village life, providing a sense of continuity with my experiences outside the classroom.

On the inaugural day at Sunrise School, the classroom buzzed with energy and teemed with new faces. The students faced a shortage of chairs and tables to accommodate everyone. Amid this bustling environment, I discovered that friends from SIS, enticed by the proximity, and perhaps curiosity, had also transitioned to this new setting, significantly expanding my circle of companions within the first year.

Sunrise School introduced me to an educational paradigm that was distinctly different from anything I had previously encountered. While the curriculum included standard classes, it was the school's innovative approach to hands-on, experiential learning that truly set it apart. We engaged in practical activities such as cultivating fruits and vegetables, planting rice, and caring for the school's cow, blending local and Western pedagogical styles. The evidence of our immersive learning experiences was visible in our clothes and shoes, which were often stained with mud from our daily adventures in this hybrid educational landscape.

Reflecting on my journey through each school, I noticed a transformative shift in how we, as students, interacted with one another. Day by day, the bonds among us strengthened, creating an environment where camaraderie prevailed and everyone was inclusively engaged in play and learning.

Two educators from this period left an indelible mark on my educational journey. Barbara, our arts teacher, played a pivotal role in nurturing my affinity for painting, especially in the realm of abstract art, a domain where I discovered my natural aptitude and passion. On the other hand, Peter, an Englishman who taught science and physical education, introduced us to soccer, instilling in us the fundamentals, strategies, and enjoyment of the game. My strong legs became an asset on the field. I could kick the ball so high and far, it would sometimes land on nearby roofs, resulting in them humorously giving me the notorious title of "The King of Breaking Roof Tiles."

These experiences at Sunrise School, with its unique educational approach and memorable teachers, significantly shaped my formative years, embedding lifelong skills and passions that they both nurtured.

Australian International School

As the months went by, I found myself moving to yet another school. A new Australian International School (AIS) had recently opened close to Sunrise School and John took me to visit it. I remember that day vividly, not just because of the school but because of John's unique presence. He dressed in his usual eccentric attire: tight leggings, a blazer over a plain t-shirt, a scarf, and for some reason, a Muslim hat — despite not being religious. His look was completed by his trademark smile. As always, he was barefoot. Whether at work or elsewhere, he carried a bamboo suitcase. This and his tiny two-seat, vintage sports car helped him maintain a consistent style that made him easily recognizable anywhere in the world.

We arrived at the school at the hottest part of the day and ran tiptoed along the pavement, trying to find shade to avoid burning our feet. I felt quite shy and uncomfortable as I noticed the curious stares from everyone around us. Heads turned to take in John's unconventional appearance, and though it amused them, it left me feeling a bit uneasy.

The concrete floors, barbed wire fence, and towering building were the opposite of the grassy grounds and mostly bamboo buildings of Sunrise School. It immediately struck me as a serious place, and I felt out of place the moment I arrived. *This is going to be a strict school,* I thought. But John's calm voice as he spoke with the teachers and principal reassured me and helped calm my nerves, even as I found myself in yet another unfamiliar environment.

Within weeks, I officially joined grade four, where I discovered there were only three other students in my class. On that first day, I took my seat among a mix of different heritages: two boys and a girl named Maya, who I am pleased to say has written a bestselling book on Balinese cooking. They all spoke Indonesian fluently, and that alone made me feel a sense of comfort and familiarity.

One of them, Fabian, was a Swiss-Indonesian boy who also happened to speak Balinese. The teachers assigned him to show me around and we quickly became close friends. Our spoken Balinese was strong, which allowed us to bond easily as we navigated the school grounds and settled into our routines. For once, I wasn't the only boy who understood and spoke Balinese; it was a relief. I finally had someone who could help bridge the language gap whenever I struggled to understand something in English.

As the months went by, more students enrolled and the school steadily grew, adding new facilities and classrooms. I found myself making more friends and my English skills steadily improved. This progress helped me feel more connected, not only at school but also at home with John and Silvia. Our interactions became a bit closer as I started understanding more about the family dynamic — who they were, what they believed in, and how they operated.

One of my cherished memories of John was seeing him return home from work early in the morning, his tiny sports car's radio blaring with music. He preferred starting work before sunrise to avoid the busy roads and traffic. I observed him at home during the day, enjoying his Marlboro cigarettes and Bintang beers, which my Balinese mom mentioned were his way to kick off the morning. Occasionally, he would call me into his room to ask if I could run to the local *warung* to buy him a few beers, sweetening the errand with, "You can keep the change." Still, my connection with John remained somewhat limited. He had no fatherly instincts like those I had felt with my Balinese dad. He lived in a world of his own, regularly disappearing into his room — his own private domain. Often, I only saw him when he'd come outside to relieve himself under the lemon tree — his favorite spot. He had an aversion to using the toilet for peeing, preferring the garden instead.

In the beginning, I was thrilled by the small reward of keeping the change from the beers. But soon, he started to give me the exact amount needed down to the penny for one or two beers, and the good days of the reward were gone. I didn't mind much that the reward had disappeared. What I truly enjoyed, and what fascinated me, was the way he'd call out from his second-floor bedroom window, shouting my name, a kind of code that it was beer time. That moment meant I'd get the chance to be in his presence, and have a feeling of connection and fun energy, a short burst of bonding.

Eventually, the morning beer errands stopped altogether and I noticed something else was changing in the house, something intangible but unmistakable. I saw John less and less and a quiet tension hung in the air.

One day, my Balinese mom noticed my disappointed look and asked, "Did you get any change?" She knew what was happening and she explained that John was running low on money. To cheer me up, she'd slip me a few coins of her own as a small incentive, sensing how much I missed those little rewards. It was her way of softening the edges of an uncertain situation that even I, at that age, could sense was shifting.

John's health had begun to visibly deteriorate. Though he remained stubbornly against seeing a doctor for weeks, he eventually got diagnosed with what the doctor's thought was pneumonia. Weeks passed and his condition worsened; the occasional cough turned into fits that left him coughing up blood. Eventually, the severity of his symptoms forced him to go to the hospital in Australia, where he was diagnosed with lung cancer. Despite the horrifying news, when it came to treatment, he flatly refused. He preferred the familiarity of home, convinced he could heal there instead, and flew back to his home in Bali.

From that point on, beers were replaced by freshly squeezed juices. Gone were the mornings when I'd head to the *warung* to buy him his morning beers. Now, each day before school, I carefully carried a fresh glass of juice from the kitchen up the steep, winding staircase that seemed to stretch endlessly to the second floor, reaching what felt like the clouds above.

It was my way of helping, though the routine had changed. This ritual became a quiet connection between us, a part of my mornings that I felt mattered in a way beyond words.

Things Moving Fast

At the age of ten, time seemed to fly as I settled into my new lifestyle. Everything changed suddenly when my sister, Made, and her French boyfriend,

Mark, unexpectedly moved into one of our houses. While I knew Made from my earlier years, I hadn't spent much time with her until then. They lived with us for several months while they searched for a place to rent.

As the months flew by, my bond with John, Silvia, Made, and Mark deepened. I began to grasp the dynamics of this family more clearly, slowly understanding who each person was and how we all interconnected. It was a time of growth for me, shaping my perspective and clarifying my place within this new family dynamic.

One day, an American man named Simon arrived at John's house. Simon was John's best friend from their days at a New York salon. A veteran of the Vietnam War, Simon introduced himself to me with a question:

"You know what this is?" He proudly displayed his nunchucks and regaled me with stories of their use in Vietnam, and his and John's past as street gangsters in their youth. Though many of his tales went over my head, I admired his cool demeanor and impressive skills, reminiscent of those Hollywood movies I'd seen. Simon was kind to me, but his tough presence made him someone I looked up to.

Simon arrived in December, just in time for Christmas. He asked me what I wanted from Santa Claus. I'd forgotten that in Italy, at the age of seven,

I'd been introduced to the concept of Santa Claus. Confused, I asked him, "Who's that?"

He explained Santa to me again and the conversation led to what I would like for Christmas. To keep it simple, I stuck to my promise of being good and asked for a remote-control car. Fascinated with batteries, I made sure to ask for one that required lots of them.

On Christmas evening, I slept on the ground floor of the house, always keeping a light on. Despite John and Silvia being just upstairs, I was still afraid of the dark. In the middle of the night, I woke up suddenly to a ringing sound reminiscent of the bells used during ceremonies by priests. My light had been turned off, but the upstairs light illuminated the garden through the large, glass sliding doors. Curious, I cautiously approached the doors to see what was causing the noise when I heard a hearty, "Ho ho ho!" Out of nowhere, a large figure in red and white clothing appeared, carrying a big sack on his back. I was so frightened that I ran back to bed.

The terror I felt may have started a few years earlier when I was playing in the gardens of Legian and saw an old man carrying a sack on his back who seemed to vanish like magic. Locals told me stories that such figures were bad and could take children away. So, when I encountered the figure in red and white with a sack that Christmas night, my immediate reaction was to run.

After sprinting back to my bed and hiding under the sheets, I heard laughter that I recognized as coming from John and Simon. Peeking out, I saw Simon's face with John beside him, both laughing at my fright. Relieved, I realized it was all a joke. Simon then presented me with a gift and they wished me a merry Christmas.

My fear turned to joy as I eagerly tore open the present. Inside was a remote-control car with just enough batteries for a few minutes of playtime. My request for money to buy extra batteries had apparently fallen on deaf ears because it never came. So, as soon as the batteries were dead, I had no choice but to retire the RC car.

One afternoon, my sisters Wayan, Made, and Ziska were visiting us, along with their respective mothers. It was the first time I would have all of them over for a sleepover, an event entirely new to me. As the youngest among us, I had no idea what would unfold the next day.

Evening turned into a restless night, and morning brought with it an increasing sense of unease, culminating in the arrival of doctors and ambulances at our home. Guarded closely by my older sisters, I was kept away from John's room. Eventually, when my sisters dispersed to visit him, I seized the opportunity to sneak a peek from his door. Inside, I saw a doctor seemingly extracting something from John's mouth with a large syringe.

Caught by a concerned neighbor who had come to assist, I was swiftly escorted downstairs away from the room. It was clear that whatever was happening was not something I should witness. I was returned to my Balinese mom amidst looks of fear, expressions I had never seen before on her or our Balinese neighbors who had gathered at our home.

Soon after, the neighbor called me back and spoke to me in Indonesian, which was translated to me in English. He said, "Luca, you must stay strong and not shed a tear. Show your dad your strength so he may enter heaven."

When I was just ten years old, John passed away at the age of fifty-eight.

Walking into his bedroom, I saw him lying on a hospital bed, looking stiff and almost like a statue. The doctors had already declared him dead and administered some sort of chemical injection to mask the smell of death. It was an unfamiliar scene and sight and I felt it couldn't possibly be John.

At that time, I didn't fully comprehend the concept of death, nor had I formed a strong bond with John. Nonetheless, I held onto the wise neighbor's advice. I didn't shed a tear — perhaps because I hadn't yet developed that close relationship with John.

According to local traditions, John's body had to remain at home for a minimum of three days. Our family and close friends stayed beside his deathbed night and day as part of the local custom of keeping the body and spirit accompanied. We slept on the wooden floors of the magnificent home he had built, with breathtaking views of the rice fields stretching as far as the eye could see.

John's passing marked the beginning of a new chapter for me and everyone who knew him. He had been the backbone of our adventures and now we all faced the need for a fresh start and a new direction.

Discussions among family members revolved around who would take care of me. It became a topic of conversation in town, with various ideas and considerations swirling around. At that time, I struggled to fully grasp the gravity of the situation we were all facing.

Amid all this commotion, another commotion was at work under our radar.

Betrayal

Pak Nyoman and John were not just business partners; they were best mates from the moment they met. John, relying on Nyoman's connections with skilled craftsmen, ventured into building awe-inspiring mansions — creations that embodied John's dreams. However, his trust in Nyoman ran deep, giving him legal ownership of all of his properties, as well as registering all of his businesses in his name due to local legal constraints that prevented foreign ownership.

Tragically, after John's untimely death, the trust that underpinned their partnership was shattered. John left behind seven ready-to-ship homes designed for Paul Mitchell's estate, a project that never materialized due to Mitchell's passing and unpaid sums. These properties, meant to be part of John's second mega build in Hawaii, and his legacy, became the center of a grave betrayal. Because there were no legal documents to prove John's ownership of the homes, Nyoman seized control, quietly claiming ownership and selling the homes one by one without the family's consent. This was a total departure from John's plans, which included selling the homes for a handsome sum and providing Nyoman with his rightful share for retirement.

The repercussions of Nyoman's actions were immediate and heartbreaking. The family, already reeling from John's loss, found themselves embroiled in disputes and severed relationships. Living with Silvia during this tumultuous time, I felt caught in the middle. Although I understood the gravity of the situation, Nyoman's household was my sanctuary, a place where I felt safe and at home, despite the unfolding betrayal.

There was no real structure to where I slept each night. Sometimes it was at Silvia's and sometimes at Nyoman's. Silvia insisted that I come back home, but I still felt out of place and was afraid to sleep alone. She had put me in the ground-floor bedroom and I would cry and scream, begging and praying to be allowed to stay at Nyoman's instead. This became a routine for some time, but as the betrayal deepened, the divide grew and no one in my family spoke to Nyoman or his family anymore. No one, that is, except me.

Nyoman made promises to me as a child when the chaos first unfolded — promises that, like the dreams of fair play and justice, sadly never materialized.

A Season of Confusion

By then, my sister, Made, and Mark had already moved out of John's house, but Made started visiting me more frequently than ever before. I vividly recall her asking me a crucial question: "Who do you want to live with until you turn eighteen — me or Silvia?"

At ten years old, confused about where I truly belonged, this decision felt monumental. It was the biggest choice of my young life, as it would profoundly shape my lifestyle and circumstances. We needed to arrange legal adoption papers due to my expiring passport, which required a legal parent or guardian's signature for renewal. This decision sparked numerous tense discussions and negotiations between Silvia and Made, like a game of tug-of-war.

With my limited experience of living with blood relatives, the decision weighed heavily on me. Silvia, who brought laughter, also intimidated me. It was daunting because I hadn't fully grasped either of their personalities yet and the choice would determine my future well-being.

I was reluctant to choose between them. Part of me wished to live with Wayan, my eldest sister, whom I perceived as the calmest and kindest. Made, while strict based on my previous interactions, was still unfamiliar to me. And Silvia had an unpredictable personality that added to the uncertainty of my decision.

Since my Balinese mom was still working for Silva, she often told me how upset Silvia got over the smallest things. It seemed like every day there was something that displeased her, whether it was about finishing the milk or using it for coffee instead of my cereal. My mom warned me repeatedly not to do certain things, like leaving the milk unfinished, because Silvia needed it for her coffee. If I wanted milk for my cereal, I was supposed to use UHT milk instead of the fresh one. These little rules kept piling up — don't do this, don't do that, or else I'd get in trouble, my mom cautioned.

For some reason, I became scared whenever Silvia came home in the afternoons on her loud Suzuki motocross bike. Because she was unpredictable, I never knew what mood she would be in. Most afternoons, she found something to get upset with my mom about — things that didn't fit into her plans or needs.

A few times, she forgot to pick me up from school, leaving me waiting until 5 p.m. until she finally arrived, saying she was either busy or had just forgotten. School ended at 2:30 p.m., so I spent several hours waiting alone, but I was never in a rush to get home anyway. In truth, if I had the choice, I wouldn't have gone home at all. It just never felt like home.

By this stage, I felt like a grown-up because I had been given a small bamboo house to stay in on the same property as Silvia, built by Paul McGregor, John's first employer from the U.S. He had come to Bali not long before John passed, presumably wanting to spend time with his old mate one last time, so he built his own little shack on John's land. To me, Paul was like a second, fun dad. He played the flute everywhere he went and chewed raw garlic like it was candy, telling me many times that he had the blood of a twenty-one-year-old.

The little house was tucked away at the farthest end of the property, a good distance from where Silvia stayed in the main house. I felt isolated and far from any sense of safety. The garden was poorly lit and Silvia had a strange love of the dark, which only added to the eeriness. At night, the jungle creaked and the wind howled, so I kept myself company with an old cassette player. I only had one tape, *Green Day*, which I played on repeat as I hid under the sheets, letting the music drown out the sounds until I drifted off to sleep.

I was caught between two worlds, where neither option seemed better than the other. Eventually, I chose Made, my sister. To ensure I had made the right choice, Made and Silvia agreed to have trial periods to test the waters. Made felt like the most natural option for me. She was only twenty-two years old with a youthful, spirited personality that I naturally connected with as a young kid.

Everything in my life up to that moment had been a blessing and a gift. My mother's passing, while a painful loss, brought me the gift of another mother who guided me into a new life, forever changing my perspective of the world and shaping the person I would become. If my birth mother had lived, I would have been blessed with her love and all the joys that others experience. I believe a higher power provides balance to one's life.

Another gift, though many might see it as unfortunate, was the passing of my father. While it's regrettable not to have known him fully and shared father-son moments, it became a blessing in disguise in the most respectful and loving way. It led me to new experiences and a new chapter in my life, prompting a shift in perspective. As I met and got to know more people, each unfolding chapter allowed me to grow and piece together perceptions. It was like seeing through a microscope, enabling me to grasp concepts,

ideas, and conversations with depth and clarity beyond what many around me could see.

New Reality

Between the ages of ten and twelve, I gradually
transitioned into a new life with Made and Mark,
moving between multiple homes.

Made was launching her Bali-to-Brazil export
business, taking on one of the most significant challenges a young woman could face at that time in her
life. At the age of thirteen, with everyone's blessing, I
made the decision to move permanently into their
rented house in Seminyak.

The location was ideal, bringing me closer to my
new school, and conveniently located across the street
from my first best friend, Tiziano, whom I had met at
SIS School. Our friendship continued at Sunrise
School. Tiziano's home was one of the coolest and
most unique homes I had ever visited, reminiscent of
John's house. It stood tall and spacious, crafted entirely from wood and straw and was surrounded by a
lush green garden teeming with a variety of animals,
from cats and dogs to even porcupines.

This move brought excitement but also a new reality check, introducing me to life lessons that would
once again shake my world. Living with Made and
Mark meant adapting to a Western lifestyle, which be-

came apparent from the moment I entered their home.

I vividly recall having to regularly sit at the table for dinner. Learning to set the table with mats, forks, knives, and other utensils left me wondering, *why so many things just to eat?* It seemed like a waste of time to me. I had to learn how to eat properly with a knife and fork, having previously only known how to eat with my hands and a spoon. Sitting there, trying to navigate using utensils with unfamiliar foods, I felt utterly lost.

Moreover, I had to adjust to eating with my mouth closed. In my previous experience, burping after a meal was a sign of satisfaction, but Mark and Made had different customs. I had to be completely retrained in these basic dining etiquettes, marking the beginning of my education in the "hard knocks" of Western norms that I should have learned earlier in life.

Mark and Made insisted that I sit at the dinner table and eat the dishes Mark prepared. Although he was a skilled cook, the food he served was completely unfamiliar to me. Salads, potatoes, and couscous presented entirely new tastes and cooking styles for my palate and I struggled to adjust, finding them difficult to stomach. Mark's strictness meant that I couldn't leave the table until I finished what was on my plate. Even when I was crying for relief and asking to go to the restroom because I couldn't keep the food down, he remained firm. It often felt like a form of imprisonment, a challenging adjustment to their expectations and culinary habits.

Mark imposed rules on me faster than I could grasp them, introducing teachings and expectations that contradicted the Balinese upbringing I knew. His approach was entirely new and unfamiliar. Being that he was ten years older than Made, Mark assumed the role of leader, dictating and directing my life according to his standards. As time passed, the situation deteriorated. Unexpected realities unfolded, turning my world upside down in ways I had never imagined possible. Mark's strict tone, especially when he spoke Indonesian or English with his French accent, gave me the shivers. Whenever I did something he didn't like — whether it was saying one wrong word or showing what he deemed "attitude" — he would grab me hard, shove me into a corner, hold me too tightly for me to move, and scream so loud that he spit on me.

My life and upbringing had been amazing until I met Mark. From day one, I grew to resent him deeply, as he contradicted the respectful environment in which I had been raised. He had no belief in the spiritual realm and showed no respect for the religious views that were important to me. This fundamental difference made our relationship unstable from the beginning, leading to many moments of conflict.

In retrospect, I understand. Until now, I've mainly shared challenging memories from my time living with Mark. It's important to recognize that memories, especially those from childhood, often emphasize the negative unless we consciously focus on the positive. At that age, I was innocent yet evolving, trying to understand a new way of life. Being taken from Indonesia and placed in a setting with Western values required me to relearn and adapt to my new surroundings. However, without acknowledging and respecting my past experiences, there was a risk of creating friction and causing me to long for separation from the relationship.

Fear is a gateway; it marks the edge of our knowledge. It teaches us what we are ready to learn, proving that where ignorance ends, courage begins

When Made and Mark decided to move to a beautiful beachfront home in Canggu, it felt like a dream in many ways. It was situated right behind a grand temple with ocean views that stretched across an untouched surfing beach. I had my own room, separate from the main house but attached to the kitchen; a space all to myself.

I was still uneasy sleeping alone, especially in the dark. Mark and Made often said I was old enough to be on my own, so I tried to brave it out — lights on, lying under the blanket with my eyes peeking out at every creak and sound. For years, I told Mark and Made that we needed to cleanse the house, but they brushed it off and didn't take my concerns seriously.

Our house staff, locals familiar with the area's stories, often shared tales of the spirits nearby — not to frighten me, but to remind me that the spirits were there to protect us, as long as we lived in balance with them. Still, feeling haunted by spirits made me afraid. There was the black figure in the mirror that appeared while I brushed my teeth. My heart would race, and I'd have to fix my eyes on the floor for a long second, holding my breath until I could look back and find it vanished. But nothing prepared me for the nights when the bed began to shake by itself. I'd get so scared that I would jump up and run to the exit, my bed still shaking. It wouldn't stop until I left the room.

I convinced a local friend from the neighboring community, an older boy who didn't mind humoring my fears, to sneak over and stay with me some nights just to keep me company. My sister eventually saw my neighbor leaving my room one morning, which led her to ask if I was interested in boys. But I told her the truth: I couldn't sleep because something was disturbing me. The night spirits kept me awake, leaving me exhausted and foggy headed each morning. Even then, she didn't quite believe me.

Eventually, my Balinese parents began visiting more regularly in the afternoons, bringing small offerings with them, and I started leaving my own as well. This made a significant difference right away; the energy in the house seemed to settle a little, but the black shadow in the mirror persisted.

A few months later, when Mark's mother came to visit, I was moved from my room to a small side bedroom with Made and Mark so she could spend the night in my room. The next morning, she seemed overwhelmed and sleepless as she recounted how a tiger had visited her during the night. She heard it growling near the bed, keeping her awake until dawn, when it finally padded off in the direction of the temple. Hearing her story, Made and Mark finally gave some credence to my experiences, providing proof that perhaps what I'd sensed all along wasn't just in my head.

My relationship with Mark improved somewhat. He was a skilled seaman and craftsman, and he played a pivotal role in shaping the life skills I carry with me today. His wisdom and teachings have deeply influenced my heart and knowledge.

Among the many things he taught me were surfing, crafting surfboards, kitesurfing, fishing, driving, and fixing motorbikes and cars — and these hobby skills were just the beginning. Mark also imparted invaluable lessons on attitude, life principles, the importance of friendships, culinary arts, respect, and love. Although I didn't fully appreciate it at the time, his guidance touched every aspect of my early teenage years. Despite this, our relationship was often marked by clashes; I never saw him as a father figure and his authoritative manner sometimes made me feel like I was under his ownership.

Unbeknownst to me, Mark was grooming me to become a man. He persisted despite my lack of interest because he knew he was teaching me important life skills. I am grateful for his insistence; without him, I would never have learned these basic skills, which my sister couldn't have taught me.

Made remained more of a sister figure during this time and didn't exert the same control over me that Mark did. She was deeply immersed in her work as an export agent in the fashion industry and was also venturing into her own fashion label. Constantly on her flip mobile phone, she managed business calls one after another. Finding a moment to talk to her was nearly impossible due to her heavy workload.

The collapse of the Twin Towers in New York on September 11, 2001, profoundly impacted her export business, leading to its downfall. At just twenty-three years old, the pressure on her to earn money and support both of us must have been immense.

After the tragedy of the 9/11 attack, Mark decided to seek a job offshore because his boat building business was slow and couldn't sustain the lifestyle they desired. He found work as a diver on the oil rigs, which meant he would be away for several weeks at a time. I cherished those periods because they allowed me to move around the house more freely, without the constant presence and scrutiny that came with him being home. Moreover, Mark's absence provided me more opportunities to spend meaningful time with my sister. During these times, I was able to strengthen our bond and get to know her beyond her role as a guardian.

However, these times with her were also tinged with stress. The financial support from my Italian grandparents mainly covered my school fees, but the other expenses of raising a child in a foreign country were a constant strain and a significant challenge that Made faced daily.

In addition to that, because I was on a six-month visa, those expenses arose every six months. I had to travel to Singapore for this purpose, which was the closest and most cost-effective option.

My earliest memories of traveling to Singapore for visa purposes are linked to trips with Mark. We made several journeys there together and he knew Singapore like the back of his hand, taking me to hidden spots, local markets, eateries, and places where the locals frequented. Each time we flew there, Mark imparted small but invaluable lessons. He may not have even realized it at the time, but these lessons have stuck with me over the years.

As a young teen, the opportunity to travel by plane so often was transformative, as that route became second nature. I learned to navigate airports, flights, and all the little details of travel that are easy to overlook. However, what made these trips most impactful was Mark himself. He had a natural inclination to share his knowledge, regardless of my age. He was determined to pass on his experiences, insights, and skills in a way that made travel feel like a deeper adventure, an immersion into the pulse of a place.

His insights were undeniably valuable, guiding us through unfamiliar places and people. However, his opinions were often bold, sometimes brash, and not always ones I agreed with. I learned to listen and observe without necessarily accepting his views as my own, developing my own sense of discernment along the way. Those silent moments of divergence, where I respected his viewpoint but held my own, were part of the deeper lessons I carried with me as we explored the world together.

A simple adventure can create memories that last a lifetime. On one of our trips, I wanted to buy a video camera, inspired by my Italian grandparents, who had documented my younger years on film. I aimed to capture life in the same way they had, preserving moments for years to come. During our travels, Mark taught me a lot about cameras — the specifics to look for and, especially, how to negotiate in the vibrant, haggling-rich environment of Singapore. Living in Asia, bargaining was part of daily life and I often listened as others engaged in this "dance of conversation" with sellers. However, doing it my-self felt entirely different.

There I was, just a young teen, moving from shop to shop in search of the best deal, each stall lined up next to the other in the bustling marketplace. I was determined to find a camera that combined quality with good value, especially since Mark was buying one for himself as well. It became a playful challenge between us — who would strike the better deal for the best specifications.

My grandmother had been sending parcels since John passed, sometimes once or twice a year, filled with branded clothes and some euros. I would open each package and be overwhelmed by the scent that clung to everything inside. It felt like being trans-ported back to Italy, as the smell instantly brought back memories of the times I'd spent there. With the euros, I learned how to exchange foreign currency into Indonesian Rupiah and began to understand con-version rates, always holding out for a better rate when I could. I had been saving up for that cam-corder for quite some time.

Mark ended up with a sleek digital camcorder, while I chose an older model that used tapes but boasted better specifications. In the end, the challenge favored me; Mark's camera broke within six months, while mine lasted for years, capturing many beautiful moments. I now have these recordings, small trea-sures from my younger years, all sparked by the idea that I could document life's moments, just as my grandparents had done for me. That small adventure became a lasting memory, a testament to the lessons learned and the timelessness of capturing life.

AIS

My time at AIS spanned grades 4 to 7. Each year brought advancements to the school, including new classrooms and the introduction of a computer class. In my first computing lesson, we learned basic tasks like starting and shutting down a computer and navigating with a mouse. At that early stage, I couldn't see the relevance of computers and found the classes incredibly dull. While I had seen my family use computers for emails, Microsoft Word and Excel, numbers and letters didn't interest me, so I didn't pay much attention to the potential that computer skills could offer.

Teachers play a crucial role as mentors in shaping our perspectives and skills. However, if a teacher doesn't illustrate the possibilities, it's easy for students to lose interest or fail to see the value in what they're learning. If only my teacher had approached the class differently, perhaps emphasizing the future possibilities of computers and how they could lead to lucrative opportunities. Engaging us in a group project or activity that harnessed the potential of computers might have captured my interest and motivated me to learn more.

Academically, I struggled in school, often receiving Ds and Es. To mitigate distractions, I made a habit of sitting in the front row of each class, hoping to listen more attentively. Despite my efforts, I found it difficult to excel even in subjects I somewhat preferred. I was constantly filled with questions for my teachers because I struggled to grasp the logic behind their teachings.

> *One word of kindness can light a lifetime's path.*

Mr. Dean, our fourth grade teacher, taught most subjects and imparted two valuable lessons that I carry with me to this day. One day during physical education, as I struggled with stretching due to my lack of flexibility, he noticed I wasn't trying hard enough and was giving up on trying to stretch further. He came up to me, looked me straight in the eyes (which made me feel uncomfortable as no one had ever come that close before) and said, "Luca, never give up." Those words touched me deeply and changed the way I approached things from that day onward. It was a transformative moment that sparked a shift in my thinking and encouraged me to explore new ideas.

The second valuable lesson wasn't something he directly said but something he shared with us as a class. Once a week, we watched something educational, and one documentary captured my attention deeply. It started slowly and I didn't understand where it was going at first. However, Mr. Dean, being one of the teachers I looked up to, paused the video at intervals to express his views and ask questions, ensuring we grasped the concepts being presented.

The documentary that left a lasting impression on me was called *What the Bleep Do We Know?* It introduced fascinating concepts in the realm of quantum physics. It made my mind wonder about all the superstitious ideas and concepts I had encountered in my young journey. As a child, I often drifted off in daydreams like many others my age. During those moments, I processed everything around me, questioned it, and engaged in my own internal dialogue.

One particular day in Mr. Dean's class, when he introduced us to poetry, I grasped the concepts quickly and wrote a piece about John's ashes that came very naturally to me. I remembered touching his ashes at the crematorium. I suppose I just wanted to be close to him, and couldn't believe that this pile of gray ash was him. I poured deep emotion into that piece, expressing feelings I didn't even realize I knew how to articulate. I don't think Mr. Dean expected such depth from any of us and he seemed genuinely surprised by how we all responded to poetry. We spent weeks writing, and each student eventually created a small, bound booklet of our own poems. When the day came to read them aloud, I made Mr. Dean tear up, and unexpectedly found myself tearing up too, overcome by emotions I couldn't quite explain.

I've carried those two valuable lessons with me since the day I learned them, guiding me through every terrain and every part of my life. It's a testament to the impact great teachers can have. Mr. Dean, your words and ideas resonated deeply, even with a student like me who never excelled academically.

Although I felt like the odd child and sometimes made fun of myself, I managed to befriend all the kids in school. I had a natural affinity for those who didn't quite fit in, and who wore their differences like a badge they couldn't hide. These were the kids who didn't have the "right" clothes, who had quirks that set them apart, and who were often targets for bullies. I recognized something familiar in them, a feeling of being outside the mold. Maybe it was my past experiences, or my sister Ziska's steady influence at school, always standing by my side to protect me. I felt I had an obligation to do the same for others who seemed to have no one to lean on.

Having come from a Balinese school where there wasn't a concept of "bullies" or "groups", the stark division between cliques at AIS surprised me. Back in Balinese school, there was no hierarchy and no exclusion. For me, it was natural to speak with everyone and hang out with anyone who wanted company. I didn't see why people needed to be separated or judged for being themselves. If someone was labeled "weird" or "uncool," I'd be the first to sit by them during breaks, to share a laugh, or just to let them know they weren't alone. I tried to be that friend who could bridge the gap and make unity a reality.

Of course, the "cool kids" saw me as a bit of an outsider too. I was aware they thought I was strange, the odd one out, but it didn't bother me. I knew I was different, and in a way, I embraced it. I was conscious of the opinions people held about each other and knew how isolating that judgment could feel. For me, it wasn't about fitting in; it was about ensuring that no one else had to feel like an outsider.

A Young Lesson on Relationship

When I was thirteen, a new student joined our eighth grade class — a girl named Liz, who seemed like royalty to us. She was Greek, stunning, and quickly became the most popular girl in school. All the boys had eyes for her and we shamelessly flirted with her every day, despite knowing we didn't stand a chance. She knew exactly how to play along, tossing back just enough attention to keep us all on our toes, making us suffer in the best way.

By then, most of the other kids already had those iconic brick Nokia phones, the ones you could actually text and call with, and I knew I needed one too. How else was I going to keep up with Elizabeth outside of school? It was a matter of survival.

Here's the part I'm not exactly proud of. One day, while waiting outside for Silvia to pick me up from school, I spotted a phone lying on the ground.

Without thinking, I picked it up and showed it to the security guard at the entrance. He took a quick look and said, "I think I know who owns it, but you should keep it," before demonstrating how to turn it off and swap out the SIM card. He even explained how that would prevent the owner from tracking it down. Some security guard! Talk about putting a fox in charge of a henhouse.

On the ride home, I wrestled with guilt. I knew I shouldn't keep the phone, but the thought of finally having a way to text Elizabeth was hard to resist. Back then, a phone like that was worth around $300 — not exactly pocket change to a kid.

The next morning, after some serious back-and-forth in my mind, I decided to go for it. I took some of the money I had saved from my mom and asked my driver - a local man who was hired to drive a rental car we had - to stop at a shop on the way to school, where I bought a SIM card. It wasn't too pricey, but the credits for texting and calling? Those added up.

To be cautious, I left the phone at home during the day. The last thing I wanted was for anyone at school to see it and recognize it, especially if it belonged to one of the students.

That afternoon, once my SIM card was installed and the phone fully charged, I felt like a new person. I was on top of the world, finally equipped with the means to message Elizabeth, who I now called Liz. I sent her my first text and from that moment, we were off. We texted back and forth endlessly, diving into all sorts of conversations and getting to know each other better. We'd keep going until one of us ran out of credit, then start back up as soon as we could reload.

After months of flirting, I worked up the nerve to ask Liz to be my girlfriend. We were at a bowling get-together on a Friday afternoon. She said yes! All I could think about was kissing her, and I had a perfect plan in mind. There was a party happening that evening, so I asked her, "Are you coming to the party? It's just across from your place."

She hesitantly replied, "Maybe, if my mom lets me."

I felt confident her mom would say yes. It was a reunion party for old friends who had all ended up in different schools. As soon as I got to the party that night, I texted her, "Come on, we're all here!"

But the response I received was, "No, my mom wouldn't let me."

My heart sank. I tried to convince her to ask again, to plead with her mom just this once, but nothing worked. It was clear she wasn't coming.

Disappointed but not ready to give up on my plan for the night, I decided I was going to make something happen. The thrill and energy were still there and I couldn't shake the idea of getting my first kiss, even if it wasn't from Liz. At thirteen, that longing felt like a fire in my chest. Determined to plant one on someone that night, I went off to see where the evening might take me. Only the first day in a serious relationship, and I was already looking for a piece of fluff on the side. I have no alibi. Such was my mania.

I found myself next to a group of girls and right beside me was Mia. She had a quiet, calming vibe that instantly drew me in. We'd never met before, but we ended up talking for hours, covering everything from random stories to my current situation with Liz. I kept a close eye on the time, though. My sister, Made, would be coming to pick me up soon and I had a mounting, almost desperate feeling that I needed to kiss Mia before the night was over.

Then, out of nowhere, it happened. We started kissing, and before I knew it, we were lost in that moment for what felt like forever. By the time I glanced at the clock, I realized it was late and I had to leave in a hurry. My sister was strict about punctuality and she'd probably already be waiting outside. Sure enough, as I made my way out around 7:30 p.m., there she was. My heart was pounding — I was late, and on top of that, I'd had a beer and I was terrified she'd notice.

Speeding away on the back of Made's motorbike, I felt a strange mix of excitement and regret. I knew right then that I'd have to break things off with Liz. I'd tried so hard for months to make that connection happen, but things with her just weren't going anywhere. I'd finally had my first kiss with someone, but it wasn't the person I thought it would be.

I spent the weekend in a fog, feeling guilty and unsure how to handle the fallout with Liz. I didn't message her, partly because I was upset that she hadn't made it to the party, but also because I was anxious about how to explain myself. By Monday morning, she beat me to it. She walked up to me and said, "I heard what happened. This relationship is over." I didn't even get a chance to explain. But honestly, she was right to feel that way and I was somewhat prepared for it.

I thought maybe I'd have a chance to start something with Mia, but then reality hit: I didn't have her number and rumors had already spread that I was a cheater. By the time I finally caught up with her, she'd heard the gossip and was no longer interested.

And so, that was my first "official" relationship — if you could even call it that. It was also my first real lesson about cheating and how quickly things can turn. The whole experience left me with a mix of regret and understanding. It's funny how some lessons hit harder than others, especially when you're young and still figuring things out.

Frequenting Italy

My world grew wider with each holiday spent in Italy, when my grandparents flew me to their home every year for Christmas. Starting at the age of thirteen, I began making the journey alone, a long flight from Bali to Italy. It was an opportunity that few other kids I knew had, and it opened my eyes to so much. Each year, I learned a little more about my family roots, how to ski, and even picked up some Italian.

In December, my cousins were still in school, so my days were mostly spent with my grandmother, Dadong, while Mr. P went to work as a sales representative. Dadong and I fell back into the familiar rhythm of our errands and daily routines, just as we had since I was seven. Nothing in the village had really changed, yet it all seemed more beautiful as I began to understand and appreciate it more.

The first time I saw snow was like a fairy tale come to life. Every morning, my Dadong would wake me up in a flurry of excitement to announce, "It's snowing!" I'd gaze out the window, mesmerized by the white world that seemed straight out of the movies. Experiencing a white Christmas wasn't something I'd ever imagined could be real, and yet there I was, living it.

When Christmas finally arrived, it brought what would become some of my happiest memories. My Italian family gathering, hugs and excitement at seeing each other again, the house bustling with laughter, music, and endless plates of food. To my eyes, the table looked like a feast fit for royalty. Food was heaped in generous portions, enough to feed the entire village, with an assortment of sweets that seemed almost magical in their abundance and variety.

Because of the warmth of family, the joy of opening presents, and the indulgence of delicious food, I found myself counting down to these holidays each year. It was more than just a vacation; it was a connection to my roots, a magical tradition that blended family, culture, and the wonder of experiencing something new each time.

CHAPTER IV

Navigating Change and Challenges

Dyatmika School

Another challenge presented itself: money. Since John's passing, my grandparents had been funding my schooling, but halfway through grade 7, that support ceased. One afternoon, Made pulled me aside after school to inform me that I wouldn't be able to continue the next term unless I used my small inheritance from Grandma Jean to cover the fees. It was that or no school at all. Faced with what felt like the only option, I chose to finish the year at AIS.

Tensions flared soon afterward, and phone calls and arguments between my sister and our grandparents dragged on. I saw the stress building in her and felt her frustration. In a moment of emotional overwhelm, she hinted — almost like a gentle form of blackmail — that maybe I'd be better off living with my grandparents in Italy. But that was never a reality I could envision for myself. My mind was filled with questions, regrets, and what-ifs. One thought, in particular, kept circling: if only Nyoman hadn't taken those homes and sold them behind our backs, we would've had the money for school. That was the moment I began to understand something I hadn't before — what money can do to people. It marked the beginning of a new awareness, a quiet lesson about life, trust, and the small things that shape us.

In 2004, I switched to a more affordable school, Dyatmika, which was even farther away, in Sanur on the southeast side of the island. The journey was no small feat: on a good day, it took over an hour and a half to get there, with luck and decent traffic. Made chose Dyatmika for me because of its curriculum and the value of its GCSE certification, which would make a difference when I graduated.

The school fees were more manageable than those of other schools, allowing us to hire a driver to take me back and forth, a common setup for students there.

Always strict about my safety, Made insisted I travel by car; she didn't trust others to drive me around on motorbikes. At the time, Mark owned a VW Safari, which became my ride. I'd pull up to school in his quirky VW convertible, feeling like I had a unique, cool setup. But then I'd see other kids arriving in BMWs, Mercedes', and even the occasional Ferrari. My ride earned a lot of laughs — kids loved to poke fun at what they called my "rust bucket," which sometimes conked out on the road. However, the teasing didn't bother me much, especially after something my driver told me:

"What seems bad to us could be saving us from something much bigger."

That line stuck with me. Over time, I began to appreciate that old car. It felt grounded, like a strange kind of protection. Sometimes, when the Safari broke down, we would later pass by the site of an accident up the road and I'd silently thank fate that it hadn't been us. Sometimes, the quirkiest things in life turn out to be the safest.

Dyatmika was a fascinating blend of students, with peers from local Balinese families and mixed families from all over the world — Chinese, European, American, and more. This diverse mix created a unique environment where I was constantly learning about different cultures just by observing my classmates. I found myself intrigued by their backgrounds, watching closely and picking up pieces of their stories and traditions.

After Balinese and Indonesian, English was my third language. For many of my classmates, it was their second, while for others, their first. This language diversity taught me a lot — not just about English but about the power of language to bridge backgrounds. We often used three languages throughout our daily interactions, adapting words and phrases from multiple languages, which enriched each day. The cultural variety at Dyatmika extended to every conversation and friendship, constantly teaching me new ways of seeing the world.

Lunchtime was one of the moments when my classmates and I got to know each other best. For some, it was easy to order meals from the catering service, but I felt it was too much to ask from my sister. Lunch from the school canteen was a luxury I couldn't justify. Since ten meals over a fortnight cost nearly half a month's salary, I decided it was better not to ask her.

As I watched my peers eat, I noticed they rarely finished their lunches. After they were done, I'd ask if I could have the leftovers rather than let good food go to waste. In the first week, my classmates laughed and joked about it. But by the second week, the most popular and wealthiest kid in school handed me his lunch, saying, "Here, Luca. I'm not going to eat this and I don't want it to go to waste." The next day, another classmate followed suit, saying, "I understand now why you don't order lunch. I saved a bit of mine to share with you."

Word of my circumstances spread, and over time, my classmates developed a quiet respect for me. What began with a few laughs evolved into genuine gestures of humility and care from my peers. Their kindness stayed with me, and that mutual respect lasted throughout our school years.

Before and after school, just across from the parking lot, there was a little *warung* run by a local family who welcomed us with their snacks and conversations as if we were family ourselves.

If we arrived early because of easy traffic or we had to wait for our drivers to pick us up after school, we'd head to the *warung* to pass the time. In the mornings, some of us would have a second breakfast — maybe a fried banana or a packet of mee goreng — instant noodles, a favorite Indonesian staple — washed down with black coffee and occasionally a takeaway Red Bull to bring into class.

The *warung* became our little hideaway, a place for us kids to test boundaries, a space of early independence and small rebellions, where we were free to just be ourselves. This was where I tried my first cigarette at around thirteen. The older boys smoked there and soon enough, sharing a cigarette with my driver became almost routine. In Indonesia, smoking cigarettes doesn't carry the same stigma as it does elsewhere; it's just part of the culture, so for us as teens, it wasn't a big deal.

Legian Beach

Learning to surf during a school activity at AIS school really kick-started my journey of getting to know the ocean and its waves. When we moved to Canggu, my afternoons were spent paddling out on a boogie board with local kids, playing in the dark sands of the neighborhood beach. The black sand felt different from the bright, inviting white sands of Kuta, and Canggu Beach had a strange, heavy energy. The dark water obscuring the seafloor gave me a feeling of unease, but it was balanced by the calm I felt while gazing at the massive temple right on the shore, where ceremonial offerings floated out with the tide. Sticking close to the shore, I still enjoyed the thrill of boogie boarding, even if I kept my distance from the more mysterious depths.

On weekends, my true escape was Legian Beach. My Balinese brother, Made, had landed a job there renting surfboards, selling Coca-Cola, and setting up beach chairs for tourists. So, on Saturdays and Sundays, I would make my way there on my own, either traveling 12km each way on my bicycle or taking the two-and-a-half-hour walk by the beach, eager to spend the entire day surfing and soaking up the beach vibes. My sister, Made, and Mark rarely left early enough to take me to Legian for the best surf hours.

Since I didn't own my own surfboard yet, my brother Made always lent me one for the day, and the waves there were just right for beginners like me. I never asked my sister for money, bringing only a few bottles of water and the Nokia phone she'd given me strictly for emergencies. She'd remind me each time to be home before dark. At the beach, my brother always made sure I was well-fed and hydrated, even slipping me a bit of pocket money. Though I insisted I didn't need it, he knew the truth and wouldn't take no for an answer. I'd stretch that money carefully, saving up for the next weekend, though chocolate snacks usually got the better of my self-control.

During those weekends, I was a full-on beach bum, spending my days surfing and hanging out. I started inviting friends to meet me at Legian instead of at my house. I thrived outdoors, finding more comfort on the open beach than in any indoor activity. Soon, Legian Beach became our main hangout, a natural meeting spot for my friends and me, with the little beach bar as our regular backdrop, our little pocket of freedom.

We surfed, snacked, and talked, free from the watchful eyes of parents. Some of us became so skilled at surfing that we helped out as part-time lifeguards, casually keeping an eye out for anyone in trouble. I lost track of how many times we helped someone back to shore. Others joined us just to relax, watch the sunset, or chat. Eventually, our crew grew so large that we would take over most of the beach bar's chairs, transforming it into our weekend haven for good times and new adventures.

Lifeguard Duties

Legian Beach was a natural classroom where I learned to read the ocean's complex languages — its currents, tides, and unpredictable shifts in wave strength. As surfers, we developed an instinctual vigilance, often spotting and rescuing swimmers from swift currents, sometimes even before the lifeguards could identify the dangers themselves.

One sunny afternoon, after a fulfilling day riding the waves, my friends and I had just showered and changed and were lounging comfortably on the sand. As we basked in the gentle sun reminiscing about the day's adventures, I noticed three locals wading boldly into the ocean. They were fully dressed in jeans and shirts, which struck me as unusual. These were precisely the kinds of risky behaviors we often kept an eye on — our own form of "lifeguard duty." Given the vast area the official lifeguards had to monitor, it was common for some areas to lack immediate supervision.

As Fabian, a close friend and fellow vigilant observer, and I watched these swimmers venture further out, we noticed a sudden shift in the current. The ocean's mood seemed to darken and we braced ourselves for action. I was midway through changing back into my surf gear just in case they needed help when I saw them begin to struggle against the water's pull. Their distress was clear even from a distance and I knew immediate action was necessary.

I glanced around frantically for lifeguards, but none were in sight, unaware of the peril unfolding before us. Driven by instinct and an urgent need to help, knowing that every second counted, I ran toward the water.. As I plunged into the surf and swam to save them, I realized that, in my haste, I had forgotten my surfboard — the only device that could aid me. I had to decide which swimmers to save first. I paused and scanned around me for Fabian. He was not far behind, paddling vigorously toward me on his surfboard. Turning back to the swimmers, my heart sank as I saw two of them, their eyes rolling back, disappearing beneath the water.

My adrenaline surged and I swam to reach the last struggling swimmer. "Stop flailing!" I shouted, managing to turn him around and prop him against my chest to keep his head above water.

Just then, Fabian arrived with his surfboard. "Two went under," I gasped out to him. Without hesitation, he plunged his hand into the water, miraculously pulling one of the submerged swimmers out by the hair onto his board. At that moment, a lifeguard finally arrived, diving in to retrieve the third person.

Exhausted and struggling against the pull of the ocean, I began frog-kicking toward the shore, supporting the exhausted swimmer with all the strength I had left. The shore seemed impossibly far, but as despair began to grip me, I took a chance and felt below with my foot. Miraculously, I was only knee-deep in water. With the last of my energy, I dragged us to the safety of the sand, relieved but drained, the reality of our narrow escape settling in.

I heaved the man onto the dry sand and immediately noticed another man with an imposing camera setup. Distracted and weary, I barely registered his presence until I positioned the swimmer safely on his side. That was when the surreal nature of the scene hit me. Several Australians, cameras in tow, sprinted toward us, their actions choreographed like a scene from a film. Before I could fully grasp the situation, they took over, attending to the man I had just rescued.

As Fabian and I stepped back, bewildered but relieved that the three swimmers were breathing, the reality slowly dawned on us: these were the Bondi lifeguards, known from the popular Australian TV show, filming a season right here in Bali.

A week later, friends reached out to tell me they had spotted us on the Bondi Beach TV show on Australian Television. The broadcast portrayed the Bondi lifeguards as the heroes who had saved the swimmers. Despite the skewed narrative, my primary concern was reassured by the announcement at the end of the episode: all the individuals involved had survived. That was all that mattered to me. The recognition was trivial; the real victory was the lives we had saved that day on the beach.

Legian Beach was my happy place and I had never felt the need to invite friends to stay over. It wasn't just that; I was ashamed and afraid of what might happen with Made and Mark, who were unpredictable. One minor mistake could turn my world upside down in an instant, much like my life with Silvia. Watching my friends interact with their parents, I saw a level of comfort and openness that was completely foreign to me. They could express anything and everything around their parents, while I felt constantly on edge, trying to avoid any confrontation.

There was one moment that reinforced this feeling. My sister picked me and a friend up from school one day. As we crossed an intersection, I tapped the hazard light button. She erupted, shaming me with harsh words that terrified both me and my friend. Humiliated, I decided I would never let my friends see that side of my life again.

Only Tiziano, my childhood friend, had glimpsed this before. Back when we lived in Seminyak, he was the only one who occasionally came over. But he genuinely enjoyed family time, while I felt an unrelenting urge to escape from mine. As we grew older, our paths diverged, partly because of this difference. I missed countless opportunities to go to friends' houses, which implied reciprocal visits to mine, out of fear that the smallest misstep could lead to harsh consequences in front of my friends.

This fear had taken root in my early teenage years, leaving me with a lost sense of self. Legian Beach became my only identity, my haven. Surfing, playing with friends, and heading back home was the extent of my life. I craved freedom to go to a friend's house or a party without facing a barrage of questions from Made and Mark, and without the constant tension. Even the smallest things that my peers took for granted felt like enormous obstacles to me. I felt like I was in a cage, constantly watching my steps, all while that deep desire for freedom simmered inside me.

The first bold step toward independence came when I planned a double date. We were about thirteen at the time, with my new girlfriend and my best friend, Rhys, whom I'd met during my years at AIS. The plan was simple enough: head to the movies. To keep Made off my back, I told her I'd be sleeping over at my Balinese mom's house. Then I called Rhys and told him to meet me at my Balinese parents' place so we could take my dad's motorbike together.

My Balinese parents were far more laid-back than Made. They held to the Balinese belief that kids need space to learn on their own, so they trusted me to make my own choices within reason. I'd ridden my dad's 125cc motorbike down to the beach a few times before, just a quick six hundred meters down the road, but I had never taken it onto the highway. In a rush of excitement, I asked if I could borrow the motorbike to go to the movies, and to my amazement, they agreed without a second thought.

Rhys arrived and we jumped on the motorbike. I took the driver's seat, helmets loosely strapped, and we hit the road. Soon enough, I was speeding down the highway at ninety km/h, the wind whipping around us, Rhys clinging to the back seat, yelling, "Slow down! Slow down! You're going to kill us!" His over-the-top fear only made me laugh. I pushed the bike faster, fueled by adrenaline, barely avoiding other vehicles along the way. Somehow, by sheer luck, we made it there in one piece.

After the movie, with no specific curfew hanging over my head — something I would have had if Made were around — we wandered the mall, basking in the freedom of the night. Then my phone rang. Made's voice exploded over the line, furious. She had somehow figured out I was lying and suspected I was up to no good. Unable to handle the lecture, I hung up, brushing it off. I told Rhys what had happened and we decided to make our way back, figuring we could deal with the fallout later.

But Made was already waiting at my Balinese parents' house when we arrived, ready to drag me back home, furious and determined to "teach me a lesson." She scolded me in front of Rhys, my Balinese family, and anyone within earshot, making me feel, once again, completely shamed and misunderstood. That night, as I felt my sense of self slip away under the weight of her expectations, I made a silent vow to never put myself in that situation again, but deep down, I knew this clash of identities was far from over.

I began pushing boundaries more, taking every chance I could to explore the freedom I craved. I often managed to sneak out at night, meeting friends at clubs whenever I could and occasionally, arranging to stay at my friend Hadi's place. Hadi was a couple of years older than I was and one of my closest friends from AIS. He was the only one among us who didn't live with a parent. Being partially adopted by an Australian family gave him the rare freedom to attend an international school and live independently.

On those nights at Hadi's, smoking and drinking beer became part of our routine before heading out. However, drugs were something I steered clear of — too many stories of bad trips and addiction had made me wary — and we felt lucky that the typical vices like hard drugs weren't common in our circle. Occasionally, magic mushrooms made an appearance, which were still legal back then. For us, these nights were about the thrill of stepping beyond the limitations of our daily lives, carving out moments of independence that felt, even then, like a kind of coming-of-age freedom.

My days were filled with glimpses of a life just out of reach, a freedom without worry I saw others living, a life I craved more and more each year. I felt the weight of each year as I waited to turn eighteen, hoping it would be my chance to finally break free. While I felt caged, restricted to a narrow path that Made seemed intent on keeping me on, the world around me seemed filled with endless possibilities. My sister and I grew further apart with each passing month. Our relationship, once one of mutual respect, became tense and strained as I grew older and longed for more independence. Every step I took toward freedom felt like a battle, as if I was constantly pushing

against her rules and the reality she wanted for me —
a reality that felt increasingly small.

Career Path

As much as I enjoyed the beach bum life, reality
soon caught up with me. When I was thirteen, Mark
posed a serious question: "Luca, what do you want to
do when you grow up?"

I was taken aback — I honestly didn't have a
clue. Up to that point, I hadn't thought about it,
partly because I didn't even know what anyone in my
family did for a living. Not even Mark.

Sensing my lack of direction, he continued,
"Maybe we should put you to work over the next
school holidays. You'll work for free, but in return,
you'll learn something valuable. Maybe you'll get a
sense of what it's like to work and start to figure out
what direction you want to take."

This was a moment that confronted me with the
reality of making choices for my future, a future that
until then had felt distant and undefined.

I hated the idea of working during the holidays.
School breaks were my time to surf all day, hang out
with friends, and escape any sense of obligation. But
that year, during the mid-year school break, I started
an internship with Warisan, Bali's well-known furniture manufacturer, owned by Silvia's new partner,
Lucio. Mark explained that with Lucio's acceptance of
me for this work experience, I would receive ten thou-

sand rupiahs — less than one U.S. dollar — per day as lunch money. That was the deal, or so Mark told me.

However, I never received that money. By the second day, I was lucky to have some leftover beach money from my brother, Made, and I had to spend it carefully to make it last. During the first week, I often barely ate throughout the day. When I did eat, it was all about budgeting. I could get a simple plate of rice with a couple of small sides — just enough to keep me going. My go-to was the little *warung* next door, where I bought whatever I could afford for just a few cents.

The *warung* owner noticed my daily visits, and loyal to her tiny shop, I spent whatever I had on food. Over time, she began adding a little extra to my plate, showing a quiet generosity that made those two weeks easier. It was a small act of kindness, but it felt like a lifeline during those long workdays, especially because I was still figuring out what the concept of "work" even meant.

Lucio assigned me the task of updating the price tags on every piece of furniture in the showroom. Knowing I had terrible handwriting, I took my time, writing each tag slowly and carefully to ensure it was legible. What could have been a quick task stretched across almost an entire week. I worked six days a week, Monday to Saturday, just like everyone else.

Each day, Mark would drop me off and pick me up, and the hours felt long, like months packed into days.

But there was one part of each day that I looked forward to: lunchtime with the security guard, who quickly became my friend. During breaks, I'd show him simple but effective card tricks I'd learned from Silvia. To my surprise, he was thoroughly impressed by my basic sleight-of-hand skills and thought I was some kind of magician. Watching him light up each time reminded me how easily the eyes can be deceived, and how reality can shift depending on the angle we see it from. He never figured out how the tricks worked, and maybe that was part of the joy for both of us — experiencing wonder in small things, even if just through a simple illusion.

In my second week, Lucio gave me access to the large designers' table and encouraged me to get creative — to sketch and dream up whatever designs came to mind. I felt a spark of excitement; this was a chance to bring my ideas to life with the help of the skilled craftsmen around me. I worked on sketches, pushing to develop an idea, but by the time anything truly took shape, my two-week stint was over and it was back to school. My designs were left unfinished, eventually tossed away with the scraps.

When Mark asked how the experience had gone, I told him honestly that it hadn't been much fun. The work felt slow and nothing had quite come of it. But as time passed, I found myself drawn to something

I'd watched repeatedly — a documentary on war photography that Mark had given me on DVD. The rawness of those captured images resonated deeply and I began to feel that photography might be my calling. I wanted to be in the field, capturing reality with the same intensity and perspective.

One day, I finally went to Mark and told him, "I know what I want to do. I want to be a war photographer."

With a nod, he replied, "I know just the guy for you." That guy was Pipping, a veteran surf photographer and journalist who ran *Magic Wave*, Bali's premier surf magazine. Pipping didn't just give me a seat; he gave me the keys to the kingdom. He told me to learn every department, to ask every question I had, and on day one, he pressed a digital camera into my hands. My mission was simple: walk Kuta Beach and document whatever I saw. It wasn't a job — it was an education.

The timing was a trial by fire. It was the week of Bali's Food Festival, and I was sent out into the chaos to capture the event for the editorial. My confidence hit a wall when it came to the prose. *A journalist?* I thought, *I can't even write!* Pipping quickly realized that while my eye was sharp, my pen was weak. But he didn't let me off the hook. He persisted, pushing me to keep writing, holding onto the hope that the words would eventually catch up to the images.

When the festival ended, my holiday — and my time as an accidental journalist — wrapped up with it. I reported back to Mark with a bruised ego regarding my writing, admitting that the "journalist" title didn't quite fit. I was a man of images, not adjectives. But despite the struggle with the prose, the experience had been transformative. I had walked into that office with a narrow dream of war zones, and walked out with a professional perspective on the grit, the deadlines, and the sheer stamina required to capture life through a lens.

In the weeks that followed, Mark introduced me to Christopher Leggett for the first time. I was thirteen. He was an old friend of my parents whom I had never met until then. From the start, Christopher seemed to know exactly who I was. During our first meeting, he asked why I wanted to pursue photography and I didn't hesitate. "I want to be a war photographer, capturing moments."

Christopher smiled and said, "I'm not a war photographer, but I can teach you photography. In return, you'll help me out for free." We shook hands and agreed. A new chapter was about to begin.

From that day on, Christopher took me under his wing. A couple of times a week after school, I'd go to his place, where he taught me the fundamentals of photography and editing. He even lent me one of his prized cameras — a big, heavy piece of equipment, far more advanced than anything I'd handled before.

The camera felt like a precious relic in my hands. I cared for it like it was made of glass, stunned that he trusted a young teen with something so valuable.

Christopher's teaching style was thorough, often resembling a classroom lecture, with his rapid-fire English sometimes leaving me feeling lost. It reminded me of being back at school, trying to grasp a subject that felt just out of reach. But things changed once he let me hold the camera and begin experimenting. Turning the dials, adjusting for light and focus, and actually capturing images — these were the moments that brought the lessons to life. It took a few days of trial and error, of bad shots and blurred frames, before I finally managed to get the light just right. I quickly realized how different it was to actually "do" the work rather than just hear about it.

When it came to editing, though, I found my rhythm right away. I loved the process — tweaking and perfecting each image, watching as small adjustments brought an image to life. Editing felt natural, like something I had been doing all my life.

Christopher was as unique as his teaching style. He had a way about him that wasn't easy for everyone to adapt to; he demanded the best at all times and tolerated nothing less. There was a toughness to him, similar to my sister, Made, a standard that made people either rise to the occasion or run away. From insight shared by his household maids, who'd watched many of his past assistants come and go, I quickly understood why he had that reputation. Taking their advice to heart, I decided to embrace his high standards without complaint, adjusting to his personality rather than resisting it. His approach taught me as much about resilience as it did about photography.

After mastering the basics, Christopher began training me as his camera assistant. I soon found myself working in fast-paced environments like events, weddings, fashion shoots, and real estate projects. The work demanded absolute efficiency, accuracy, and timing. I had to learn to anticipate his needs — what he wanted and when — before he even reached for something. It was almost like mind-reading, but with the precision that only came from understanding his style, preferences, and rhythms. I had to adapt to his flow, predicting his next move and being one step ahead at all times.

The only regular outlet from the restrictions of living with Made and Mark came when I was working with Christopher. The nights when we worked together became my escape, a way to see beyond the walls of my limited world. Through these gigs, I learned valuable skills in photography and the demands of good work ethics, but I also had the rare chance to experience the island's animated nightlife scene. Working with Christopher was a glimpse into a different life, filled with laughter, lights, and the energy of people who seemed to have the very freedom I desired. For a few hours, I could pretend I belonged to that world too. But every time I returned home, the cage I felt around me became even more apparent.

Over time, Christopher and I developed a smooth, efficient two-man team. The fast pace and constant need for accuracy excited me; I loved the challenge. Timing and efficiency were at the heart of everything Christopher did. Every second counted because each moment had the potential to capture the exact shot he needed. I learned quickly that success in photography often comes down to capturing "the" moment — a split-second where lighting, expression and movement align perfectly.

Christopher was well known as the "photography king" of the island, with a reputation for perfection and relentless dedication. His guidance shaped me deeply, teaching me to work not only with skill but also with the right attitude, agility, and respect for the craft. Through the years with him, I didn't just learn photography; I learned discipline, fast thinking, and adaptability. The experience of working under Christopher's intense, meticulous eye gave me my first real taste of work I could be passionate about. In many ways, those early years shaped me, fueling a love for photography that would become a core part of who I am.

With the skills and knowledge I gained from working with Christopher, my first year as his assistant opened up new opportunities. Gradually, I started receiving requests from family and friends to shoot small gigs — sometimes for free just to build experience, and eventually for modest pay. With only a basic camera and a macro lens Christopher had given me, I had to make do. Shooting groups of people with a macro lens was challenging, to say the least, but it taught me to work creatively with what I had. Looking back, I'm amazed at what I accomplished with such minimal equipment.

Earning money doing what I loved filled me with a deep sense of purpose. Photography became a way to contribute, a form of expression, and a source of freedom. The experience gave me an appreciation for the process and instilled a gratitude that would stay with me long afterward. Being able to create something meaningful — and even make a living from it — felt like the start of a new chapter.

Crossing the Line

> *Traditions are to be kept, learned, and adopted; otherwise, you will fall out of place.*

Legian Beach, where we often encountered familiar faces and made new friends, was essential for expanding our social circles beyond the confines of school. Gustra, a high-caste Balinese boy from Dyatmika School, had become one of my best friends. He was dating a half-French, half-Indonesian girl, which frequently brought us into the orbit of the French expatriate community, a group that typically kept to themselves. I received an invitation to a birthday party from a French girl who had seemingly developed an interest in me during our beach gatherings.

The invitation served as a bridge between distinct social circles, drawing us into a setting that was unfamiliar yet intriguing, illustrating how interconnected relationships could lead to new social opportunities.

However, the party atmosphere changed dramatically within the first hour as tensions escalated between Gustra and some French boys. The evening had started pleasantly as I mingled with the girl who had invited me, but it soon became clear that underlying hostility existed. Gustra found himself surrounded by a group of French boys who began hurling insults and threats at him. The situation quickly intensified, disrupting the initially relaxed environment.

Urged by the girls to take our dispute outside, Gustra and I stepped into the dimly lit street, where my frustration boiled over. The disrespect shown to Gustra by the French boys, fueled by jealousy over his girlfriend, was unacceptable to me. In the heat of the moment, I drew a pocket knife, a recent gift from Mark intended for fishing. With the blade in hand, I confronted the group, which had swelled to more than ten against the two of us. My display of the knife finally commanded their attention.

"Put the knife down!" one of them yelled.

"Afraid to fight fair?" another said.

"It's already not fair. I'm just balancing the scales," I challenged. "Who wants to bleed first?"

I was hoping they would buy my bluff because I was just as worried about actually stabbing someone as they were about getting stabbed. I struggled to keep my face expressionless and inscrutable, but my heart and mind were raging storms. In an instant, I saw myself from a distance and wondered who I had just become, pulling a knife like some street hoodlum. In the next, I saw myself as an old man in a prison cell, being given a life sentence for multiple murders. But I was determined to protect Gustra at all costs.

"Well?" I demanded.

There was a pregnant pause when all of them seemed to be considering whether or not this situation was important enough to warrant possibly seeing their own intestines for the first and last time. Sensing their fear, I lunged at them, doubling down on my cold-blooded killer act.

Thank all things holy, most of them decided that they liked their blood right where it was, and retreated against the wall, with some even leaping over a nearby stream in their haste to escape my fury. But a few stayed, probably worried about hating themselves in the morning if they ran.

As I held them at bay, local guards from the nearby community center, alerted by the noise, emerged to assess the situation. Gustra explained the altercation to them, and amidst this tense standoff, the observers found humor in the fright of the French boys. Under the watchful eyes of the local community, the boys eventually issued a begrudging apology to both Gustra and the local guards, acknowledging their mistake.

After that fiery confrontation, I found myself reflecting on how deeply the situation had affected me. I had frightened them, and in doing so, I had also startled myself. Following that night, whenever those French boys encountered me, their demeanor was markedly different. They treated me with unexpected kindness, as if the event had instilled in them a respect not only for me but also for the cultural norms of the land they were visiting. It was as though they realized they had crossed a boundary of respect and decorum required in a place that was not their own. This shift not only restored peace but also reinforced the importance of understanding and honoring local customs and community spirit wherever one might find themselves.

Birth of Lily

All within the same year, and shortly after Made discovered she was pregnant, Mark was diagnosed with bone cancer. It was a time of mixed emotions — incredible excitement about the baby on the way tempered by deep concerns and a lingering tension. Mark, true to his determined nature, continued working offshore to keep up with the bills, right up until the last month before the baby's arrival.

In 2004, at just twenty-four years old, Made gave birth to their daughter, Lily Jean, in an at-home water birth. I remember the evening vividly. My task was to keep making hot water in the kitchen and running it back to her water bath, ensuring it stayed warm. It was a small but important role that gave me a sense of responsibility and excitement. I felt like I was part of something incredible. The birth of Lily Jean was like gaining another sister, and it was a beautiful, defining moment for me as much as it was for our whole family. I thought to myself that one day I too wanted to have a family as young as they were.

I had never seen Mark as happy as when Lily was born. With purpose and devotion, he set to work preparing the house for his daughter's safety, applying rubber around every edge and corner she might one day stumble upon. His diagnosis had shifted something monumental within him, transforming his once-military-grade toughness into a phase of discovery and learning, a complete shift from the man I had known before. It was as if a light switch had been flipped on, revealing a softer, more introspective side I had never seen.

During this time, Mark became like a man on a mission, dedicated to getting better and doing all he could to witness his family grow. His perspective on life changed so profoundly that I, too, found myself drawn into his journey of self-betterment. He embraced his own evolution with an urgency that was inspiring to watch.

Despite being an atheist, he turned to meditation, silent retreats, and various healing classes. He pursued every form of healing and transformation he could find, driven by a deep desire to survive this terrible disease and be there for his family. He was a man fighting for time, and his fierce commitment left an impact on everyone around him.

Around this time, my Balinese brother, Made, introduced me to Reiki and meditation, powerful practices that quickly became transformative parts of my life. We joined classes together, where a local master taught us without charging a fee, inviting anyone open to learning. I began to understand the depth of human energy and the healing potential within each of us.

Within months, our group started hosting free community healing sessions on Legian Beach, where anyone could stop by for relief from discomfort. It was unlike anything I had experienced before, performing what felt like miracle healings for those in need. After hours of healing sessions, I felt entirely drained, yet I was filled with an undeniable belief in the power of human energy and the connection we shared with those around us.

The conviction that these practices could help Mark grew stronger within me. I believed I could heal him if he embraced the energy work. I told him he had to believe in both of us and in the power of the energy that would flow from me to him; it wasn't about my personal ability to heal, but about allowing the natural energy of our surroundings to support his healing.

He reluctantly agreed to one session, but I sensed he was skeptical and we never repeated it. I hoped he'd open up more with time, but the belief just wasn't there. Meanwhile, neighbors began hearing about my healing abilities and word spread quickly through the area. Occasionally, as I passed through the neighborhood, someone would stop me, requesting a small healing. It was remarkable to realize that even as a young teen, I could offer something so meaningful to others, even if I couldn't yet help the one person I truly wanted to heal.

During this period, Made was still working for another company, exporting clothes to Brazil, but after 9/11, the business took a serious downturn. The economic shift pushed her to reevaluate her future, especially now as a stay-at-home mom after Lily's birth. She began pouring herself into her long-held dream of becoming a fashion designer. Day by day, she worked on her designs at home, slowly building the vision she had held for years.

With Lily as her inspiration, Made took the leap to create her own women's fashion line. She eventually opened a manufacturing factory and launched her first shop, naming the brand "Lily Jean" in honor of her daughter. Through dedication and resilience, her vision came to life and Lily Jean began its journey as a unique brand with personal meaning and a deeply rooted story behind it.

Witnessing Made and Mark work tirelessly every day and facing the struggles that accompanied it instilled in me a strong sense of self-reliance. I began to understand that by asking for less, I could lighten their load, allowing them to focus on the many responsibilities they juggled. Conversations around the dinner table often turned to money — food expenses, health insurance, the cost of flights to Singapore every six months to renew our visas, and countless other essentials. These discussions were eye-opening, and I became acutely aware of how each dollar seemed to be stretched.

One vivid memory I have is when Made introduced me to cereal. It was a luxury because it was an imported product, and the price tag reflected that. I could see how even small comforts came at a significant cost. The concept of "enough" became deeply ingrained in me, and this lesson on the value of money would stay with me for years to come.

Mark's Passing

After Lily was born, we had to leave our beachfront house in Canggu behind. The peaceful ocean view was replaced by the noise and flashing lights of

Old Man's nightclub, which had taken over the area, and the late-night music was growing louder. Mark, still fighting his battle with cancer and caring for a one-year-old baby, decided it was time to find a quieter place away from the chaos that was beginning to dominate the beach as it gained popularity.

They found a new home in Berawa, just five minutes inland from Canggu Beach. The house had a simple, traditional Balinese layout. Mark, with his many skills, transformed the space. He added new wooden decks, painted the walls, and prefabricated the floors, giving the house a more homely and spacious feel. It was a testament to his dedication to creating a comfortable space for us, a place where we could find some calm amidst everything happening around us. Mark was incredibly skilled and resourceful and he poured his energy into making that house a welcoming new home.

As we settled into the new house, I was given a room just big enough for a single bed and a small table. Unlike my previous one with its glass doors, this one allowed me true privacy. At sixteen, that privacy was something I deeply valued — a place where I could close and lock the door, and finally have a sanctuary of my own. In my little haven, I could freely express myself. I started painting the walls, filling them with colorful, abstract designs — my own canvas for whatever I felt like creating. It became a space where my artistic mind could run free.

By then, Lily was around two years old and had a room of her own, though hers was bigger than mine. That didn't bother me. I liked the smaller space; it felt safe and close, almost like a cocoon. Growing up in small rooms over the years had made me comfortable with a cozy, contained space.

Since the beach was now a fifteen-minute bike ride away, my sister and Mark granted me the privilege of driving their 4WD jeep in the afternoons to go for a surf. There was one condition: I had to fill the tank myself. Fuel was fairly cheap back then, but the jeep was used only occasionally, so it was usually running on fumes. I would drive to and from the beach only when I had enough cash to fuel it up, which became my first priority. It gave me a sense of ownership and pride, and something about that rugged jeep made me feel a little cool. The five-minute drive to the beach became my little moment of freedom, a taste of independence and adventure all my own.

As the months passed, Mark's health deteriorated rapidly. His body grew weaker by the day, reduced to mere skin and bones, and he was consumed by pain. I would hear him cry out from his bed, his voice raw and filled with anguish, "Give me a gun. I can't take this pain anymore."

The cancer had ravaged his bones, leaving him in relentless agony. He had stopped chemotherapy months before, unable to withstand the toll on his already frail body, and had turned to alternative, natural remedies in the hope of relief.

Watching him suffer was something I struggled to endure. I felt a deep, complicated regret welling up inside me. I thought of all the curses toward him I had uttered in anger over the years, and guilt settled like a weight in my heart. More than anything, I felt sad for Lily, knowing that she might grow up without her father, just as I had. It pained me to think she would face the same reality I did — a childhood shaped by absence and loss.

One afternoon, I came home from school to find Mark lying unconscious in bed, the pain finally too much for his body to bear. The doctor told us that he could still hear us, even though he could no longer respond. The weight of that knowledge — the idea that he was trapped in silence, listening yet unable to speak — hit me with an emotional force I had never felt before. I stood there, watching my family gather around him in reverent silence, feeling the presence of the inevitable. I knew he could go at any moment.

In that instant, I decided to confront the shame I had carried over the years. I needed to have a private moment with Mark to say what I felt, to express the unspoken thoughts I held, in case this was my last chance. I leaned close, speaking to him, hoping that somehow he could hear me and understand. Overwhelmed, I left the room, tears spilling from me in a way they never had before.

Only minutes later, Mark took his last breath.

Teenage Years

Months after Mark's passing, I was eager to push past the familiar shores of Legian Beach. Watching my friends venture into clubs and house parties, and zip around on mopeds with complete freedom, I wanted that same rush, that same taste of independence. But the tight boundaries set by Made still held me back; I wasn't allowed to do this, couldn't do that, and was always limited by her rules and expectations. The only option left was to bend a few rules and challenge my fears of my sister's reaction.

I was neither a risk-taker nor a rule-breaker by nature; my experiences up to that point had made me cautious. The thought of landing myself in more trouble wasn't exactly appealing. But as I got older, the need to experience life the way my friends were stirred inside me, sparking ideas I'd never dared to entertain. Those glimpses of freedom in my friends' lives pulled at me, tempting me to confront the fears that had held me back all along.

One evening when I was just shy of seventeen, Made took me to a newly opened beach club right behind my Legian Beach hangout. For the first time, she allowed me to drink some alcohol. As the dance floor came to life, I felt an exhilaration I hadn't felt before. Dancing freely, my heart raced with the energy of the music, and as if it were a moment meant to be, an

Australian girl around my age joined me on the floor. We danced, kissed, and exchanged numbers, which led to the start of a long-distance relationship. She was from the Gold Coast, and soon we were texting, calling each other, and feeling that teenage rush of young love across the miles.

After a few months of this back and forth, Made noticed my interest and asked if I'd want to visit the Gold Coast during the December holidays. The trip, she suggested, might even open doors for studying there one day. Inspired by the idea, I researched universities and sent out applications, hoping to secure an appointment while I was there. Although I received no replies from the schools, the plan to visit Australia became my focus, and my anticipation built as December drew closer. When I finally landed in Brisbane, the reality of being in my "half-country" hit me in a way I hadn't expected.

Passing through customs was a strange experience; despite holding an Australian passport, I was met with questions as if I were a complete foreigner. The officials asked why I was entering, leaving me confused and a bit fearful, feeling as though I'd done something wrong. After a tense moment, they let me through and I found myself finally stepping into a world that felt both familiar and foreign.

Those two weeks on the Gold Coast were filled with adventure, exploration, and a sense of discovery I hadn't known before. I spent days with my girlfriend, wandering along beautiful beaches, exploring zoos, and learning about the Australian way of life. I saw young adults living independently, taking on jobs, and pursuing education, which opened my eyes to a place where growth felt possible and accessible for people my age.

Upon returning to Bali, I experienced a renewed sense of motivation and a longing to live life on my own terms. The more I watched my friends freely chasing opportunities and making their own choices, the more restless I became, feeling confined to the sidelines. As my desire for independence grew stronger, it felt like every inch of freedom I tried to claim backfired in some way, leading to more trouble with Made. She still held tight reins over what I could and couldn't do, and as a teenager, I wanted nothing more than to break free of those restrictions.

For example, Made allowed me to take her Vespa, but only for short rides down to the beach or to nearby day clubs where she and her friends often hung out. Even that limited freedom gave me a taste of what I craved.

One day, I was heading back from a quick stop at a small shop, riding within the "approved" distance, when out of nowhere, a group of teenagers on motorbikes came speeding down the hill from the opposite direction. Before I had a moment to react, one of the boys lost control and his bike skidded straight into mine, sending me airborne and slamming me to the ground.

Miraculously, I walked away without a scratch, but the Vespa was completely ruined. The boy who'd caused the accident had the nerve to blame me for the damage to his bike. Shaken and a little dazed, I called Made to explain what had happened, thinking she'd come to help me sort it out. But instead, she erupted on the other end of the phone, yelling, "This is your mess. Fix it. I'm not paying for anything."

Nice to know you've got my back. Thanks loads! I said to the disconnected phone.

The boy's parents soon showed up, taking his side, and suddenly I was surrounded by people blaming me for the crash. I was alone in the middle of the street with no witnesses other than the group of kids who were siding with him. I felt trapped. They couldn't get any money from me, so eventually they all left, leaving me to face the aftermath on my own.

When Made arrived to pick me up, she was furious, treating the whole ordeal as though it was my fault.

"This is all your fault," she said. "Your precious need for *freedom* is only bringing more chaos into our lives."

Each time I tried to prove I was ready for more independence, it only seemed to pull me further back, reminding me how far I still had to go before I could make my own choices and stand on my own. The incident left me questioning if I'd ever be trusted enough to truly have a say in my own life.

As year eleven ended, my teachers had a candid conversation with my sister and me about my academic path.

"Progressing to year twelve might not be productive given your struggles with year eleven exams," one of them said, implying that exams in year twelve would likely prove insurmountable for me. So, I set my sights on Australia, planning to pursue studies in arts and photography — something I truly loved doing.

Meanwhile, my relationship with Made grew increasingly turbulent. At seventeen, I was still forbidden from going out, staying out late, and riding a motorbike — restrictions that my friends didn't have. Each rule she imposed felt like a wall, pushing me to find ways to test her boundaries. I became more cunning and determined, and found myself standing up to her with a fierce resolve. I was ready to challenge her, to finally claim the freedom I craved.

Dunkan's Pink Palace

One day, after an explosive argument, Made kicked me out. I knew I had driven her to severe frustration with my rebellion, but at that moment, I also saw a kind of freedom waiting for me. I packed a small bag with my essentials and photography equipment and made my way to Dunkan's rental unit in Legian. Dunkan, Nyoman's eldest son from his first marriage, felt like family to me. Nyoman's new wife never accepted him, so Dunkan was raised by his mother alone. He worked at the beach like my brother.

Everyone in our circle knew Dunkan as the "gangster" of the nightclub scene — he was well connected, knew everyone who mattered, and the clubs in Kuta were his playground. Whenever I sneaked out, just knowing Dunkan was around gave me a sense of safety.

Dunkan's place was modest, with walls painted a distinct shade of pink, which earned it the nickname "The Pink Palace." My Balinese family understood the strict environment Made held me to, so they didn't bat an eyelid at my decision to move in with Dunkan. His place felt like a haven, a space to breathe and redefine who I was becoming.

Around this time, I had finally saved enough to buy a vintage motorbike. I earned the money working with Christopher and from my own photography gigs at nightclubs, and often at the venues where my sister Ziska went with her friends. I had a steady stream of income, making enough in a single week to live comfortably for a month, sometimes even earning more than the local average salary. The opportunities Made had given me with Christopher, along with life lessons from Made and Mark, had provided a solid foundation and the independence to create a life for myself. Living with Dunkan, I felt the beginnings of a life that was entirely my own, supported by work I truly enjoyed and a sense of freedom I hadn't known before.

Dunkan's little place quickly became the center of my new world. My nights at the Pink Palace were filled with friends he'd met from the clubs, both guys and girls, along with music, drinking, smoking, and nonstop party energy. It was everything I'd imagined freedom would be: driving wherever I wanted, surfing when the waves called, going out to nightclubs, and getting my first tattoo to mark this new era. It was a drawing of my mom on the left side of my chest. I was living fully in the life I'd dreamed of — or so I thought.

Then one day, out of the blue, my sister called me for the first time in months. She told me I would soon need to handle my own visa situation and life insurance, which meant leaving the country, as was the routine every six months. She asked if I would come back home to figure it out. Her call made me pause and think seriously about what I wanted next. My girlfriend on the Gold Coast came to mind; we were still together and I hadn't strayed from her despite my newfound independence. The endless cycle of partying, late nights, and freedom was already starting to feel stale. The rush of doing what I wanted, when I wanted was wearing off, and I found myself wondering, "Is this really what I'm after?"

I talked to my stepmom, Silvia, who offered to help buy me a one-way ticket to the Gold Coast, and even gave me a $100 US bill to get started. In a month, I was set to fly out, with no real plan beyond staying with my girlfriend until I figured things out. I had no job lined up, no money beyond the $100, and no clue where I would earn more. But somehow, I wasn't worried. Up until then, I had made my own money, supported myself, and managed to get by.

Looking back, I realized just how much self-confidence, or maybe sheer youthful boldness, I was running on.

Photo Gallery

Berate & Luca

Luca In Balinese School

Luca In Balinese School

Luca & Daniela

Berate, Luca & Daniela

Luca & Marta

Ziska, Wayan, Donaldine, Made, Luca, John, Marta &
Jean

Marta

Luca & Ziska

Ziska, John, Silvia & Luca

Made & Komang

Luca, Komang, Berate & Made

Marion & John's Engagement

Marion & John

Hawaii Construction

Ziska & Donaldine

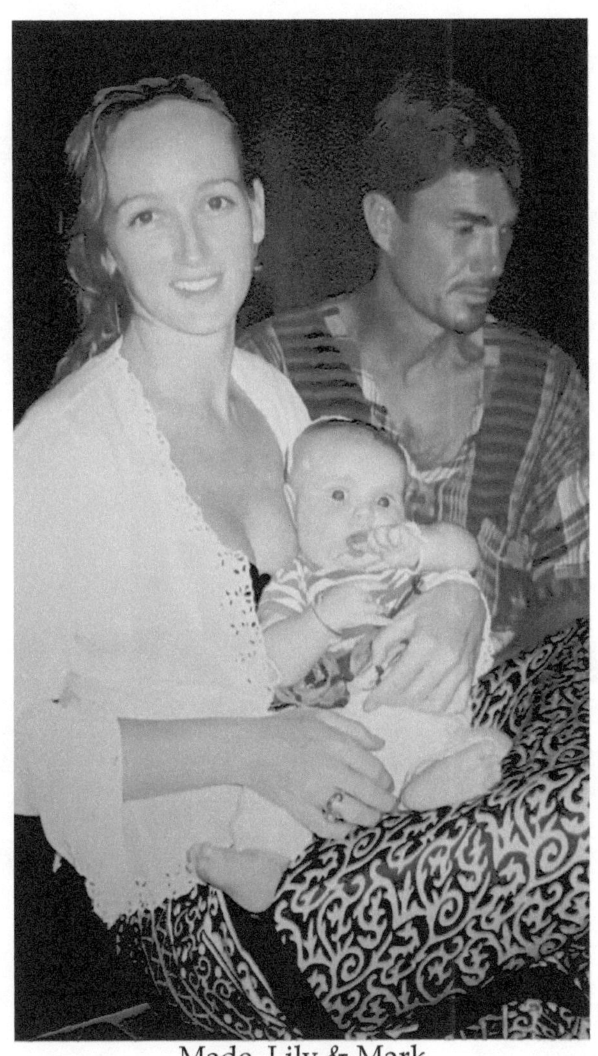

Made, Lily & Mark

John & Marta

Luca, Silvia & Ziska

Silvia, John & Donaldine

Berate, Luca & Nyoman Dayuh

Luca, Ema, Eli & Annie

Anna, Eli, Ema & Annie

CHAPTER V

Breaking Cycles

A week before my flight to the Gold Coast, I received a call from my girlfriend. I had been so excited about finally reuniting with her, but in a single conversation, she told me she wanted to break up. Just like that, my whole plan was shattered. I had bought a one-way ticket to be with her, picturing a fresh start, and now I was left holding nothing but that ticket. I was upset, of course, but something in me remained surprisingly positive.

Later that evening, while drinking with Dunkan and a few of his Australian friends, I opened up about my situation. That was when Jye, a guy I had only just met, spoke up and offered me a place on his couch until I figured things out. I barely knew him, so I wasn't sure if he was serious, but as the night went on, I got to know him better and found that he was a genuine guy with connections to many of the same people I knew.

Over the next few days, I spent more time with Jye, building our friendship. By the time he flew back to the Gold Coast, I felt more confident about his offer. When I finally landed at Gold Coast Airport with all my belongings, he picked me up and took me to his place, a cozy spot just fifty meters from the beach, where he lived with another friend I hadn't met until then. I felt a mix of relief and excitement as I settled in, exploring the area bit by bit, relying on my $100 for essentials like a SIM card, bus rides, and my first stock of noodles and eggs.

This new beginning wasn't at all what I had planned, but as I stood there, fifty meters from the ocean with the sun setting over a place I had only dreamed of, I knew I was on the edge of something big.

Jye sat me down and said it was time to get things sorted, starting with setting up a bank account and getting a tax file number, two essentials if I was going to work in Australia. However, with only my passport as proof of identity, it wasn't easy. Here, people needed several documents to establish who they were, and I didn't have much to go on. Luckily, Jye's mom worked at a bank and did me an enormous favor by helping me open an account. As for the tax file number I needed to apply for a job, I had to gather personal documents such as my citizenship certificate and an ID card, which required fees to apply for. At the time, I didn't have a cent to spare, so I had to put those on hold and focus on finding a job that would pay cash in hand. I searched the internet for hours each day, sending out hundreds of applications, but nothing came through. It was a lesson in resilience and patience — qualities I hadn't fully appreciated until then.

I used so much data searching for jobs online that Jye's provider charged extra for the data usage. When he brought it up, I explained that I had no money to help cover it, still running on the last bit of that initial $100. It was around my third week and I was just scraping by. He then asked, "Have you gone to Centrelink?"

Centrelink

I had heard of Centrelink before but hadn't looked into it. When I told him no, he said something that sparked my curiosity: "They'll give you money to live on."

Surprised, I replied, "I don't like borrowing money."

But he shook his head, explaining, "No, it's not borrowing. The government provides it if you're in need, and they even help you look for work."

All I really heard was that they'd help me find work, though the idea that a government would actually provide money was almost unbelievable. Jye directed me to their office location, and the next morning, with my last dollar in hand, I caught a bus and made the long ride out. Arriving at a large, pristine office space, I joined the long queue. After standing in line for nearly two hours, someone finally called me over and asked why I was there. I replied, "I need help finding work."

At the front desk, they handed me a number and told me to wait again. Another hour passed before my number was finally called. I sat across from a woman who seemed genuinely curious, but skeptical. She began asking a series of questions, probing deeply into who I was. I felt completely vulnerable and even a bit frightened, like I was being interrogated. My only identification was my passport, and she was baffled when she couldn't locate me anywhere in the system. She started asking more questions, such as where I had come from and why I was in Australia, and my nervousness grew until I found myself telling her the whole story, bit by bit; everything that had led me there.

When I finished, she got up and walked away, dabbing her face as she moved across the room. I watched her talk to other staff members, my heart pounding and my mind racing with worry, wondering if I'd said something wrong. Soon, she returned with another woman, and to my surprise, they both had red eyes. She introduced me to this new woman and asked me to share my story again. As I recounted everything, I noticed tears in their eyes, drawing the attention of nearby staff. It felt surreal, sitting among this unexpected sympathy, while a growing crowd of staff members glanced over with expressions of pity and shock.

Looking back, I think it was my total lack of expectation that caught her off guard. I wasn't demanding a right. I didn't even know I had any. I was purely admitting total, drowning defeat. It appeared to be an office where frenzied people came armed with anger, desperation, or calculated pleas, so my raw disorientation must have revealed a different vital need that wasn't commonly seen.

When I finished, the two women exchanged looks and I was left in a long silence that felt almost unbearable. Finally, the first woman spoke, her voice calming as she typed on her screen, giving me more details than I could comprehend. I interrupted, hesitantly asking, "Will you help me find a job?"

She took a deep breath, visibly relieved, and explained everything, though the only part that stuck with me was that they'd be depositing a couple of thousand dollars into my account the next day. It felt like an unimaginable sum. She even offered me some pocket money for food that day, but I politely declined, saying, "I can wait until tomorrow."

I walked out of there in a daze — both overwhelmed and grateful but struggling to process what had just happened. The idea of receiving money simply because I was in need was something I couldn't fully grasp.

Sure enough, the money landed in my account the next day. The relief was immediate — I could finally pay Jye for the internet overuse and some back rent I owed for overstaying at his place. It was a weight off my shoulders, but I also knew deep down that it was time for me to move on. I'd been leaning on his kindness for too long and I didn't want to overstay my welcome any further.

First Australian Job

As if the universe had been listening, a miracle came my way just a day later. Lauren, the girlfriend of a friend from Bali, reached out, asking if I was interested in teaching surfing at a surf camp south of Byron Bay. Without hesitation, I said yes, my excitement barely contained. It felt like a lifeline, an opportunity to start afresh, make my own way, and escape the uncertainty that had been hanging over me.

The very next day, I packed up all my belongings, hopped onto a bus, and headed south. As the bus rolled into Byron Bay, the air shifted. This place was different — the entire place was electrified with a vibrant, free-spirited energy that felt oddly familiar, like a slice of Bali transplanted into Australia. When I arrived, Lauren met me at the local bus station and took me around town, giving me a tour of this laid-back but inspired hippie haven. It was surreal and comforting, a reminder of home yet with a unique twist of its own. After catching up on life and soaking in the vibe of the town, I boarded the private surf camp bus that would take me to my new home. This was the start of another chapter, one filled with promise, adventure, and independence. The surf camp was calling, and with it, the chance to carve out a life on my own terms.

The job was straightforward: teaching backpackers how to surf at the camp where they'd stay for a night or two before continuing their journey north to Byron Bay. For six months, this became my world. It wasn't glamorous — I earned less than $100 a week — but the camp provided everything I needed, from meals to a place to sleep, and the lifestyle more than made up for the modest pay. Days were spent in the ocean, helping travelers catch their first wave, and nights were filled with laughter, stories, and a sense of camaraderie that only the simplicity of camp life can bring.

Those months shaped my young adult years in ways I hadn't anticipated. It wasn't just about teaching; it was about connecting with people from all corners of the globe, hearing their stories, and sharing a piece of mine. The freedom, the ocean, and the constant flow of new faces gave me the feeling of adventure I'd longed for back in Bali.

But as with many good things, it ended abruptly. One day, I was called into a meeting with the camp manager and informed I was being fired. The reason? "Sleeping with the clients." While this behavior wasn't uncommon among the surf instructors — it was practically a running joke — the manager seemed to single me out. There was an undercurrent of jealousy in his tone, though I couldn't quite place why. It was a blow — not just to my job but to the sense of belonging I'd started to feel there. Though the dismissal was unfair, it became a lesson about people and the dynamics of jealousy and authority, one that would stick with me long after I left the camp.

I boarded the bus once again, this time with only $700 to my name, and headed back to Byron Bay. The owner of the surf company, despite firing me, had offered a lifeline: I could camp for free on his swampy campsite. It wasn't much, but it was something. With no other options, I spent my remaining money preparing for what lay ahead — buying a tent, warm clothes, and a few basic supplies as winter loomed. Life quickly became an exercise in survival. Each morning, I woke with the sunrise, escaped the oven-like heat of the tent, and set out to local businesses, relentlessly searching for a job.

Despite my efforts, the job hunt bore no fruit. Days turned into weeks and my funds dwindled rapidly. My meals became basic rations — canned food and slices of bread were an extra treat. As my body grew thinner and weaker, desperation forced me back to Centrelink for assistance. This time, the payments were far less generous, barely enough to scrape by. It was just enough to cover food or rent, but not both. With no other choice, I remained at the campsite, sneaking into a nearby hostel to use their showers. That small act of defiance ended when I was caught, but instead of being thrown out, I was offered an arrangement: I could clean toilets at night in exchange for camping on the hostel grounds for free. Begrudgingly, I accepted.

Each day brought a mix of loneliness and unexpected adventure. The campers around me were mostly older than I was, with their own stories of chasing freedom or escaping something back home. Despite feeling adrift, I began to find comfort in the routine. Occasionally, I bumped into backpackers I taught to surf, which opened doors to nights out at Byron's beach clubs. They bought me drinks and we stayed late into the evening, soaking in the live reggae bands. This became my weekly escape from the monotony of my tented life.

Eventually, luck intervened in the form of a former student who was also struggling to find work and housing. Together, we found a shared house seeking two tenants. The rent, just $125 a week, was manageable thanks to my modest Centrelink payment upgrade of $300 a fortnight.

Moving into the house was a small step forward — a reprieve from campsite life — but it was far from a solution. I spent my days indoors watching endless movies, eating cheap junk food, and sinking deeper into lethargy. The creativity and ambition that once fueled my spirit withered, leaving me empty. Without a job or a clear direction, life began to feel like an endless cycle of nothingness.

I avoided burdening my family with my struggles, brushing off their check-ins with assurances that everything was fine. The truth was, I didn't want their pity, nor did I know what to ask for. I was honestly lost within myself. My life had become a day-to-day existence, my mind spiraling downward with no clear purpose or hope for what lay ahead.

Perth

As I reached out to friends who had made their way to Australia, it became clear that most had settled in Perth, which was across the country from where I was. Perth was an appealing choice — it was cheaper, had a closer connection to Bali, and offered more job opportunities. Deciding to join them, I was surprised to learn that Gala, my young school crush from AIS, was also there. She was crashing on a friend's couch — another classmate from Bali who had gone to Perth for university. Gala and I quickly began discussing the idea of getting a shared place together, as she too was looking for better opportunities beyond Bali.

However, I had one major problem: I didn't have the money to get to Perth. Then, as if the universe had intervened, my Italian aunt called out of the blue, offering a lifeline I hadn't dared to hope for. She wanted to send me money for driving lessons so I could increase my chances of getting a job. Grateful for her generosity, I accepted the funds but used them instead to buy a one-way ticket to Perth. When I arrived, I stayed on my friend's living room floor, determined to find a job as quickly as possible so I could get my own place.

Not long after my arrival, I landed a job at a modern café/restaurant. Coincidentally, the manager loved my name, Luca, because he planned to name his son the same. Whether it was fate or luck, he hired me on the spot. I worked hard, earning more hours because the manager appreciated my work ethic. Before long, I was able to afford a rental nearby, which came with a second room. Fortunately, Gala was allowed to move in as well, splitting the rent with me, though the arrangement required us to share a bed. By then, any childhood feelings I had for her had faded. We lived more like siblings than anything else.

For almost a year, this was our life. I picked up a second job at Domino's to make ends meet, working over forty hours a week between the two jobs just to save up. My goal was simple: to eventually afford a ticket back to Bali to visit my family and friends.

Work became the center of my life — rushing between shifts, paying rent, and trying to eat something other than instant noodles. Although the hourly pay felt impressive compared to what I was used to, the high cost of living in Australia quickly drained my income. I worked endlessly just to keep up, with little to show for it.

Meanwhile, Gala, still on Centrelink payments, took a much more relaxed approach to life. She spent her days exploring and enjoying her freedom while I worked myself to the bone. Seeing this difference highlighted the growing disconnect between us. I wanted more than this grind, but I didn't know what "more" even looked like.

One day, I felt satisfied, thinking I was making progress; the next, I felt utterly lost, confused about who I was becoming and unsure of what I truly wanted. It was a cycle of hope and uncertainty, pushing me forward, but holding me back at the same time.

Two Years, One Choice

My relationship with Made began to reopen during this time, shifting from the strained connection we had before. She sensed my unhappiness and encouraged me to pursue my passion for photography, even offering to pay for further education. With her support, I found a photography college situated right on Sydney Harbor and soon found myself heading to Sydney, full of hope and ambition.

Through Made's connections, I landed a job at a famous photography studio owned by one of her friends. The job was anything but glamorous — I was the studio lackey, responsible for maintaining seven

studio rooms, painting, cleaning, and handling anything that needed to be done. My daily routine was
rigorous: college classes from 8 a.m. to midday and
then working at the studio from 2 p.m. until 10 p.m. It
was a grind, but I reminded myself that this was just
the start. The job gave me a foot in the door of the industry and brought me closer to high-profile photographers who used the studio space.

Toward the end of my college years, I began assisting these photographers as I became more familiar
with the regulars who rented the studio. Slowly, I felt
my skills improving, and as I gained confidence in
my abilities, opportunities started coming my way.
The studio recognized my growing talent and work
ethic, offering me various positions, from lackey to
studio manager. For the first time, I found myself
overwhelmed with choices, standing at a crossroads
that demanded careful consideration.

In the midst of these opportunities, Made called
me, asking for help. Her company was growing
rapidly and she needed someone who could bridge
the gap between her and the local workers in Bali, a
role that required both understanding and effective
communication. She painted a compelling picture of
the importance of my involvement, and her timing co-
incided with my own growing discontent with life in
Australia.

Despite the promise of a career in photography, I
felt isolated living in Australia. Making friends was

difficult, meeting people seemed impossible, and life revolved entirely around work. Photography was fulfilling, but I knew that to truly excel, I would have to go beyond assisting or managing rentals at the studio. Although I was gaining valuable experience and enjoyed my work, my current path wasn't providing the sense of fulfillment or joy I sought in my lifestyle.

> *Experience, while invaluable,*
> *can sometimes act as a barrier to growth.*

We often reach a point in a specific field where our accumulated expertise no longer challenges or excites us, leading to a plateau in our development. This stagnation marks the end of growth in that particular area. New opportunities, however, spark excitement and a desire to engage deeply, until we find ourselves caught in a familiar cycle of initial enthusiasm followed by eventual disinterest. In my journey with photography, this cycle was a recurring theme, where the thrill of learning and mastering new techniques gave way to a search for fresh challenges.

The opportunity with Made offered something different. It was a chance to develop practical skills in business and leadership. It was also an opportunity to return to the life I knew in Bali and reconnect with friends and family.

Bali had always been where I felt most at home, a place where I could roam freely without the rigid structure of life in Australia. Many of my friends who had moved to Australia felt similarly, and most had already returned to Bali for the same reasons I was now considering leaving for. We find comfort in the familiar, not in exploring new territories, which is why we often return to the security of what we know.

Weighing my options, I realized the decision was clear. But one major challenge stood in my way — a girl I had met months before, whose love wrapped my world in joy and fulfillment like never before. Her name was Wafa. She was from France. Letting go felt almost impossible because she sparked so much life, love, and affection within me. When I broke the news to her about the opportunity, she surprised me by saying, without hesitation, "I'll come with you," despite having only been in Australia a few months into her year-long working holiday.

In the end, we planned our exit from Australia to Bali, with me working for Made while she sought a job for herself. I didn't know how this move would unfold but I knew for certain that the skills I'd gain there would be just as valuable as any I could acquire in Australia. More importantly, I'd be surrounded by the people and environment that felt like home, a freedom that no career opportunity in Australia could offer me.

Leaving Sydney, with its promise of growth and opportunity, at the age of twenty marked a pivotal moment in my journey. Choosing to prioritize a new life skill over the stable yet unfulfilling path I was on was not a decision I took lightly. Reflecting on my two-and-a-half years in Australia, I see how those experiences gifted me invaluable life skills — things I might never have learned had I not taken the leap. It reaffirmed a belief that has grown stronger with every chapter of my life: An attempt, no matter how small, is always better than no attempt at all.

Taking a leap doesn't mean you have to clear the entire distance in one go; it begins with the courage to take that first step forward. Those years taught me resilience, adaptability, and the value of perseverance, even when things felt uncertain. I am profoundly grateful for those experiences and the way life seemed to unfold, often in ways that felt as though they had been written before I even lived them. It was like stepping into the script of *The Truman Show*, a strange feeling of life playing out as if it had all been planned.

Returning to Bali brought a mixture of emotions. There was an undeniable pull to return to the place where I felt most grounded, but a nagging question lingered in the back of my mind: Was I leaving to escape my new reality and future potential, or was I simply going backwards?

The future, as always, was a blurry concept for me. I didn't dwell on it or try to plan far ahead. My focus was often on the present — the current job, and the next step in my day-to-day life. The only distant dream I held onto was the thought of starting a family of my own, but even that felt like a vague idea rather than a concrete plan. I had always lived in the moment, letting life unfold organically, without questioning too much about what lay ahead. Now, as I prepared to step into this new beginning back in Bali, the same sense of trust in the journey would guide me once again.

CHAPTER VI

Back to the Roots

Working in Bali

Wafa and I found our first home together at Didi's place. For six months, that house became our base as we rebuilt our lives. She secured a job at a French company not far from Didi's and we settled into a routine with our work conveniently close to home. Meanwhile, Made and Lily lived much farther away, creating a quieter space for Wafa and I to navigate all these changes.

To enable us to move around freely, I bought my second vintage motorbike for $300 — equivalent to a small fortune for me at the time. It was an investment I made carefully, choosing to save most of my Australian earnings for future needs. The bike symbolized my independence, a reminder of the freedom I had long sought.

Starting as a Manufacturing Manager

Diving headfirst into my sister's business as a manufacturing manager was like being thrown into the deep end of a pool without knowing how to swim. Starting from scratch with zero knowledge of the industry felt daunting yet exciting. My role wasn't one I grew into gradually — I had to transition quickly, learning ins and outs of an industry I had never explored.

The irony of the situation wasn't lost on me — a foreigner managing a production line of highly skilled Balinese workers, many of whom had been in the trade their entire lives. It felt both unorthodox and controversial. Here I was, someone with no prior experience in manufacturing, tasked with leading a team of seasoned professionals who had perfected their craft over decades.

But therein lay the beauty of this challenge. I didn't come in with a sense of superiority or an attitude of authority. Instead, I approached it as a student, learning from the very people I was meant to lead. My first lessons came not from textbooks or training manuals but from observing the hands-on expertise of the workers around me. Each person became my teacher, showing me the rhythm and intricacies of the work.

I noticed the skepticism in their eyes at first, questioning my ability to contribute anything meaningful. However, over time, as I learned to ask the right questions, show respect for their skills, and roll up my sleeves to learn alongside them, the barriers began to dissolve.

This role was not just about managing production; it was about earning respect in a culture where ability and humility mattered more than titles. My willingness to embrace their skill and experience and acknowledge my inexperience became the bridge that allowed me to connect with the team.

A Lesson in Humility

Taking on this role taught me an important lesson in humility. Leadership isn't about knowing everything — it's about being willing to learn and adapt. Managing production wasn't just about output and efficiency; it was about people, relationships, and mutual respect. I also learned that vulnerability isn't a weakness; it's an opportunity to grow, to understand, and to earn trust.

Starting from the ground up in my sister's business not only shaped my understanding of the industry but also redefined my perception of leadership. It taught me to lead with curiosity, to value the insights of others, and to recognize that true strength lies in our ability to admit what we don't know. This chapter of my life, though unconventional, became a powerful reminder that stepping into the unknown often leads to the most profound lessons.

The factory was enormous — unlike anything I had ever seen before. Rows upon rows of sewing machines buzzed rhythmically, operated by more people than I could count. Their faces were focused, their hands precise, and their workspaces were a flurry of activity. As my sister introduced me to the local manager who had been running the show for some time, I could feel the weight of responsibility settling in. This wasn't just a job — it was an entire world I was stepping into.

When I left the cool office for the bustling factory floor, a wave of heat hit me like a punch. The sun blazed down on the tin factory roof, making me instantly aware of how much these workers endured to keep production running. My shirt clung to me and beads of sweat formed on my scalp. I suddenly felt the depth of what this role would demand of me.

Though I had never met the workers before, a few recognized me from years ago when they first started working for my sister. Back then, I was a young teen who used to hang around Made's tiny office after school. They knew who I was, and when they heard me speak their language fluently, their initial hesitation dissolved. I wasn't just some foreigner coming in to take over — I was someone they saw as one of their own. Their curiosity turned into comfort and I felt an immediate sense of camaraderie and mutual respect.

As the days turned into weeks, I found myself immersed in a world I had never imagined. Person by person, process by process, I began to understand how intricate and complex the work truly was. Each piece of clothing crafted there was a masterpiece — luxury handmade garments that sometimes took a month or more to complete. This was an art form, a harmonious blend of skill, creativity, and precision.

I moved from one station to another, guided by the skilled workers who were generous with their time and knowledge. They taught me their craft with patience, explaining every detail of their process like teachers guiding a student through a new subject. Their expertise left me in awe. I had always respected hard work, but seeing it up close in this way was something else entirely. It was humbling to witness their dedication. Each stitch, each cut, and each detail was part of a larger system that worked in perfect synergy.

A Full-Circle Moment

As I learned, I couldn't help but flash back to the early days when Made first started her business. I remembered visiting her tiny office space after school, watching the skilled workers she had hired create her very first line of clothing. I would sit quietly, waiting for her to finish work so we could go home. Back then, I didn't fully grasp the scope of what she was building. Now, standing in this massive factory, surrounded by a team of artisans, I saw how far she had come. The magnitude of what I was stepping into hit me hard. This wasn't just a job for me — it was a continuation of a story that had been unfolding for years, one that I was now becoming a part of in a much deeper way. My respect for Made and her vision grew exponentially as I realized the sheer effort, creativity, and resilience it took to build something of this scale. This was an opportunity to learn, to grow, and to contribute to something extraordinary.

Taking the Reins

Before I knew it, my sister had handed me more responsibility than I had ever imagined. It felt as though she had placed the weight of the entire business in my hands. I was now in charge of overseeing every process, from the largest production decisions to the smallest, seemingly insignificant details — like taking inventory of items I wouldn't have otherwise given a second thought to.

My plate filled quickly. Working six days a week, Monday to Saturday, became my reality. The stress was visible — my hair began to turn grey at just twenty years old, a clear sign of the overload I was taking on. Yet, despite the pressure, I found myself stepping up to the challenge.

Each day, I faced situations that demanded immediate attention. Every decision, every problem, and every issue that arose needed a solution — and that solution had to come from me. I had no choice but to become creative and solution-oriented, thinking on my feet and learning to navigate challenges as they arose.

This was no ordinary job; it was the real deal. There was no room for slacking or second-guessing. Each day was unpredictable, bringing new challenges and experiences that pushed me beyond my limits. It

was a relentless cycle of problem-solving and decision-making, and as exhausting as it was, it kept me
going.

The work was intense, but it was far from boring.
The unpredictability of it all — combined with the responsibility of being at the center of such a dynamic
business — gave it meaning. I was growing and
evolving in ways I couldn't have foreseen, gaining
skills and resilience that would shape me for years to
come.

As overwhelming as the workload seemed at
times, it also gave me purpose. The constant demand
for solutions and the ever-changing nature of the
work kept me engaged. It was a far cry from the mundane routines I had experienced before. Here, I was
part of something bigger, something that required every ounce of effort and creativity I had to offer.

In many ways, this role was a trial by fire, but it
was one that I embraced wholeheartedly. Each challenge became an opportunity to prove to myself —
and to others — that I was capable of handling whatever came my way. Despite the stress and the increasing number of grey hairs, I found myself thriving in
this high-pressure environment, where every day felt
like a new day in an ongoing journey of growth and
discovery.

The workers and I quickly became like family, a
necessity in the local way of working. Without that
sense of unity and respect, I would have lost them en-

tirely — they would have simply walked out. Maintaining a balance of respect was crucial. It had to be upheld every minute of every day.

As a young and inexperienced manager, leading older men and women who had far more knowledge and experience than I did was a unique challenge. I knew respect was key — this was a value deeply ingrained in me from my upbringing — but understanding it and practicing it in this new context were two very different things.

The turning point came when I made a conscious effort not to dictate their work. Instead, I prioritized building a connection with them, allowing them to know as much about me as I wanted to know about them. This approach fostered mutual understanding and created harmony in our professional relationship.

Once they saw that I wasn't there to simply boss them around but to work alongside them and learn from their expertise, everything shifted. They began to open up, sharing their life skills and teaching me nuances of the trade that I desperately needed to understand.

These were life lessons wrapped in decades of experience. Each piece of knowledge they shared became invaluable, not just for the job but for how I viewed relationships, leadership, and teamwork.

In many ways, this dynamic was a reflection of Bali itself — a culture rooted in respect, balance, and harmony. By embracing these values, I was able to earn their trust and support, and in return, they helped me grow into the role I had taken on.

Understanding Working Cultures

> *Treat each individual as a king or queen and things will change for you — for you are them.*

Having worked with both Indonesians and Australians, I noticed distinct differences in their workplace cultures. In the West, the focus often lies on structure, individualism, and direct communication. In contrast, Asian workplaces, particularly in Bali, value collective harmony, indirect communication, and respect for hierarchical structures. Another notable difference was the integration of religious practices into the daily schedule. In Bali, it's customary for workers to take time for religious exercises up to twice a day, which impacts production timelines — a concept absent in Australian workplaces and one that initially caught me off guard.

Adapting to this new style of working required a flexible approach, but it wasn't an impossible challenge for me. Having grown up speaking the native language and living among the locals, I understood their logic and working culture as if it were my own. Surprisingly, my greatest challenges didn't come from the employees, but from my sister.

The Toughest Cookie

Made was as tough a boss as she was a sister. Her fiery nature was well-known, and for me, the hardest part of the job wasn't managing the factory or navigating cultural nuances — it was managing my relationship with her.

Despite years of trying to overcome my fear of her, I often found myself reverting to the intimidated little brother under her watchful eye. However, what gave me a strange sense of confidence was realizing I wasn't the only one who felt this way. The employees, many of whom were seasoned workers with decades of experience, seemed as wary of her as I was. It was a universal understanding, an unspoken bond we all shared. Seeing them react the same way I did — nervous glances, quiet nods, and avoiding her wrath — was oddly comforting.

When things went pear-shaped and conversations turned heated, I often felt my body tense up, my thoughts scramble, and my confidence shatter. My natural response was to smile. To her, a smile was a joke, but for me, it was my only way of expressing myself. In Bali, when we get mad at someone, the response is a smile because we lack the vocabulary for this type of aggression. We also express shyness through a smile. Although her words could cut deep and the sting of being ridiculed — especially in front of others — was hard to shake, over time, I realized I wasn't alone in this experience.

While her methods were tough, they stemmed from a relentless determination to ensure the success of the business and the continuing employment of her workers that she held closely as part of her family. It wasn't easy, but it was a lesson in resilience. Working with Made taught me to stand firm, find strength in solidarity, and most importantly, to embrace the challenges that shape us into stronger individuals.

In the workplace, my sister and I treated our relationship strictly as professional, separating familial ties from our roles in the business. I had no privileges and no expectations of special treatment. This mindset was crucial to maintain, especially in an environment where familial favoritism could easily be perceived. I needed the employees to see that I wasn't a figurehead with unwarranted authority or someone leveraging a family connection for personal gain. Instead, I presented myself as someone there to learn from them, collaborate, and earn their trust as one of the team.

Lessons in Leadership

The challenge of managing perceptions taught me invaluable lessons in leadership. True influence doesn't come from authority; it comes from trust, respect, and shared purpose. When a crisis arises, a leader has a solution. By ensuring the employees felt valued and respected, I was able to create a healthier, more collaborative work environment.

Ultimately, the business remained unequivocally my sister's, both in practice and in perception. I was there as a steward, not a successor. This distinction allowed the employees to maintain their loyalty to her while also building a rapport with me. It was a delicate balance, but one that proved vital in ensuring harmony and productivity within the team.

Rediscovering Balance Amidst Chaos

The rag business consumed me entirely. Each day felt like a relentless battle against stress, sleepless nights, and the overwhelming pressure to meet endless demands. It was a world where my responsibilities multiplied and every decision carried weight. The constant struggle to keep the business running smoothly left little room for anything else, including my own well-being.

Amid this chaos, I found myself reflecting on the person I had once been — someone who understood the importance of balance, someone who once practiced Reiki and embraced meditation to center the mind and become aware and acceptant of all that came to me. I realized how far I had drifted from those practices, caught up in the whirlwind of work and forgetting the tools that grounded me and taught me acceptance.

In an effort to reclaim some sanity, I returned to meditation. At first, it was challenging to find the mental space for it amidst the daily grind. But slowly,

I began to dedicate moments to reconnect with my inner self, to breathe through the stress, and to let go of the constant worries that plagued my mind. Meditation became my lifeline, reminding me that the creation of peace was within, even in the storm of daily pressures.

During this intense period of adjustment and learning, my relationship with Wafa began to falter. The demands of the business consumed not only my time but also my emotional energy. I was stretched so thin that I couldn't contribute to our relationship in the way she deserved.

The low salary I earned compounded the strain. With limited financial means, there was no space for leisure, no opportunities for shared experiences outside of the confines of work. We became two individuals caught in the grind, with little room for joy or connection.

As much as we loved each other, I felt overwhelming guilt. I couldn't bear the thought of restricting her life, of holding her back from the opportunities and happiness she deserved. It was a harsh realization, but I knew the weight of my struggles was becoming a barrier in our relationship.

Unable to bear the guilt, I made the painful decision to let her go. But instead of explaining my struggles and fears, I chose to shield her from the truth. I told her that I no longer loved her, a lie meant to free her from the limitations I felt I was imposing on her life.

It was one of the hardest things I had ever done, especially since we had come all this way from Australia. I carried the pain of that decision, knowing that I was pushing away someone I deeply cared for. But I believed that by letting her go, I was giving her the chance to find a life unburdened by my struggles. She accepted my explanation and left with dignity, even kissing me on the cheek before she left and whispering "be happy" into my ear.

Looking back, I understand now that honesty, even when uncomfortable, would have been a kinder choice. But at that time, I was blinded by my own sense of inadequacy and the belief that I was doing what was best for her. This taught me profound lessons about love, stress, and the importance of balance. It reminded me that relationships require not just love but also the ability to share burdens and joys equally.

Reflecting and Rebalancing

Months after my breakup, I found myself sitting in the wreckage of my decisions, reflecting deeply on the events that had unfolded. Committed again to the daily practice of meditation, I took the time each afternoon to reconnect with my inner peace. With every session, I felt the layers of worry and self-doubt peel away. Over time, the gray hairs that had been a visual testament to my stress began to disappear, my nights became restful, and my mind found clarity.

Life gradually rebalanced itself. I learned to leave work behind when the day ended, focusing instead on the joy of life's smaller moments. Sunday afternoons became sacred, reserved for moments of relaxation, reflection, and gratitude. It was as if the heaviness of responsibility had lifted, allowing me to rediscover a sense of freedom and purpose.

The Hidden Wisdom of Bali

Living and working in Bali deepened my appreciation for the island's inherent wisdom. The Balinese way of life is a masterclass in balance, respect, and human connection. On this island, the concept of "understanding before being understood" is a way of life.

Through daily interactions with the locals, I came to see how naturally they embodied this principle. They taught me, not with words, but through their actions, smiles, and unwavering sense of community. It's a lesson that's often overlooked in the fast-paced, individualistic cultures of the West; it has the power to transform relationships and lives.

This chapter of my life taught me that growth doesn't always come from monetary success or ease. Sometimes it's the challenges, heartbreaks, and moments of doubt that shape us the most. Through meditation, reflection, and learning from the people around me, I began to see the world — and myself — with greater clarity. I am forever grateful for this time in my life. It taught me the importance of balance, the value of genuine connection, and the strength that comes from within when you commit to understanding yourself and those around you, as well as the sometimes unseen values we bring.

As I moved forward, these lessons became the foundation upon which I would build the next chapters of my journey.

CHAPTER VII

Building a Future Reflecting on the Past

Meeting Lucy

Within my first two years of working alongside my sister, life took an unexpected turn. I met a Slovenian woman a few years older than me at a friend's newly opened bar. She was visiting Bali on holiday and a local friend introduced us. Our connection was instant, and within a week, we started dating. By the second month, she moved in with me, marking the beginning of a new chapter in my life.

At the time, I was living with my best friend, Rhys, from AIS and his partner in a cozy Balinese-style home we had secured a few months earlier. The house was small but filled with the kind of joy and camaraderie that only close friends can share. She quickly became a part of this little family and it felt like life was finally offering me a balance I hadn't experienced in years.

One evening during our first month together, Lucy and I went out for dinner. She wore a red checkered shirt that instantly triggered a vivid memory from my teenage years — a shirt I had once envisioned my future partner wearing in a dream-like moment of my youth. Sitting across from her that night, I was struck by how surreal it felt. It was as if the universe was reminding me that some things align in ways we cannot fully understand.

As life has its own way of unfolding, Lucy and I found ourselves facing an unexpected reality. Six months into our relationship, she discovered she was pregnant. The news hit us like a storm — equal parts joy, fear, and disbelief. Suddenly, everything I had thought I understood about life shifted to deep questioning and reflection.

My first concern was financial. I was earning $500 a month, barely enough to support myself, let alone a partner and a baby. She wasn't working, her visa was running out, and I had no idea how we would manage this new responsibility. Breaking the news to my sister Made felt like facing a storm. She had always been a mother figure to me, and her reaction was a mix of concern, practicality, and hard questions about how I planned to handle this situation.

As I took in the reality of becoming a father at twenty-two, my thoughts drifted to my own upbringing. I'd wished for a young family someday, though I never pictured it arriving quite this soon. I felt both prepared and completely unprepared. Watching my sister raise Lily and reflecting on the challenges faced by many parents I had known gave me some understanding of what lay ahead. But no amount of observation could prepare me for the weight of responsibility now resting on my shoulders.

For the first time, I realized that my decisions would no longer just impact me — they would shape the life of another human being. The fear of failure was heavy, but so too was my determination to do everything I could to create a better experience for my own child than I had. This new journey gave me a renewed sense of purpose as I grappled with where I was headed in life.

This chapter of my journey was one of growth, transformation, and learning to embrace the unexpected. Lucy's presence brought challenges and a deeper understanding of myself, and the journey we were about to embark on would test me in ways I had never imagined. This was the beginning of a new life — not just for our child, but for us.

Marriage and Family

With money seeming to arrive just when it was needed most, Lucy and I decided to travel to her homeland, Slovenia, for a simple marriage ceremony and to sort out her personal matters before returning to Bali to build our life together. While I had always dreamed of a grand wedding celebration surrounded by family and friends, our finances simply couldn't accommodate such extravagance. Instead, the simplicity of our union reflected our current reality.

At the time, I viewed marriage through a practical lens. In Indonesia, documentation and bureaucracy can be a labyrinth, and being legally married would simplify the process, especially with a child on the way. It wasn't just about the paperwork, though. Deep down, I knew I wanted a family of my own one day. The idea of raising a child and building a family resonated deeply with me — a dream that had quietly taken root in my heart when Lily was born.

This wasn't how I had imagined it would all begin. In my mind, I had envisioned more time to prepare, to grow, to save. Yet here I was, about to embark on the journey of parenthood and marriage far earlier than I had anticipated. It was a leap of faith, fueled by blind love, hope, and the undeniable pull of life's unfolding mysteries.

As we stood at the threshold of this new chapter, I reflected on my own upbringing. I thought about the lessons I had learned from my family, the struggles I had witnessed, and the dreams I had carried for years. Lucy and I were about to create a new story, one that would blend her roots with mine, her culture with Bali's, and her dreams with my own.

While the road ahead was uncertain and we were still getting to know each other, I held onto the belief that the challenges we faced were shaping us into stronger individuals, and building a more resilient partnership. This was the beginning of creating a legacy, a chance to create the kind of family I had longed for — a family grounded in love, understanding, and shared purpose.

Village Life: A New Perspective

As Lucy and I prepared for the arrival of our child, we made the decision to move in with my sister, Made, up in the villages where the air was fresh. This shift was a reprieve from the ever-expanding chaos of urban Bali. The village provided something the bustling city couldn't: serenity, space, and the gentle embrace of fresh winds. It was a stark contrast to the concrete jungle, and I could feel its calming influence seep into our lives, even as the pressures of work and finances remained constant. Living with my sister offered its own set of challenges, but the support and space it provided allowed us to navigate this period of our lives without additional strain.

Still working with my sister at the time, I knew that surviving on one income wasn't sustainable, especially with a baby on the way. Determined to ease the burden and secure a better future, I took on as many photography gigs as I could. My camera became my lifeline and I seized every opportunity, shooting fashion collections, interior designs, and Airbnb listings.

The grind was relentless. My days were tightly packed, leaving home at eight in the morning to head to the factory and returning by six in the evening. In between, I squeezed in photo shoots during my hour-long lunch breaks, racing on the moped from one location to another before returning to the office. Evenings were dedicated to editing, often late into the night, as I transformed the day's raw captures into polished, professional images.

The rhythm of my life was demanding but purposeful. While the physical and mental toll was undeniable, I felt driven by the knowledge that this effort was for my new family. Each photo shoot, each edited image, and each late-night session brought us one step closer to the stability of cashflow we needed because the cost of living in paradise for a foreign couple is not always what it seems.

My Son's Birth

In January of 2014, our son was born. With his arrival, our world shifted, forming new memories and a sense of purpose. A year later, we moved out of my sister's home, giving our little family the chance to embrace more freedom and flexibility to explore what Bali had to offer.

Watching my son grow up in a similar environment to my own upbringing was like traveling back in time. Seeing him play in the same kind of surroundings and hearing him speak both the local language and English at such a young age brought me immense pride and joy. At two years old, he spent much of his day with a nanny, yet his grasp of English, something I had struggled with as a child, was flourishing.

Throughout his young years, as a family of three, life became an adventure. We traveled to various countries, taking advantage of the free flights offered to children under two. Although I hadn't envisioned these experiences, they were filled with wonder and exploration. However, amid the excitement, I began to notice things that I had overlooked during the early days of our relationship.

With the demands of work and the responsibilities of parenthood, I had been so focused on staying afloat — ensuring we had what we needed — that I hadn't taken the time to fully understand the person I had married. Slowly, the reality of our relationship revealed itself. The woman I thought I knew began to feel like someone entirely different. It wasn't a sudden change, but a gradual realization that left me feeling like both the giver and a ghost in my own relationship. I started to notice that she didn't know who I really was and I didn't really know who she was. The small things kept adding up, creating distance between us that made me feel both unhappy and fearful. I snapped back to reality, realizing that what I'd believed was real no longer held true.

Transition to Entrepreneurship

After six years of relentless work as a 9-to-5 manager, I decided to leave my job with my sister to focus entirely on an online e-commerce business Lucy and I had started. The venture was finally generating healthy profits after a few years in the making and I envisioned a life with more time with my son, wife, friends, and the simple joys I had been missing.

But reality had other plans. Instead of the freedom I had imagined, I found myself with more on my plate than ever before. The business consumed every waking moment, leaving little time for anything else. Our priorities shifted toward sustaining the business and managing home essentials. What I thought would bring balance to my life only deepened the divide between the life I had and the life I hoped for.

The idea of living in paradise slowly morphed into something less idyllic. Bali, once a place of joy and simplicity, became the backdrop to a life consumed by work and routine. Our sunsets and social interactions at Legian Beach faded into the distance as the demands of running a business took over.

Amidst the chaos, I continued to reflect on what I wanted for my son and for myself. The lessons I had learned growing up, the struggles, and the sacrifices began to shape the way I approached this chapter of my life. It was a time of growth, self-discovery, and recalibration — a time to redefine what paradise truly meant for me and my new family.

This phase of my life reminded me that balance is not something you find; it's something you create. Although upon reflection, this is simple to understand, it was another thing to apply those simple words at the time. The journey of fatherhood, marriage, and entrepreneurship was a complex and evolving one, filled with both challenges and triumphs. Through it all, the drive to build a better future for my family remained at the core.

A Hopeful Transition: The Move to Australia

Focusing on the future and our son's opportunities, we set a goal to move to Australia within a couple of years. Our vision was to provide him with better schooling when he turned five, a healthier lifestyle, and the kind of opportunities we felt would shape his future for the better. Yet, beneath this plan was a more personal and complicated layer — my attempt to keep our family together amidst the growing tensions in our relationship. I feared that without this move, she might one day leave and take my son back to her home country.

The year leading up to this transition was a battle. I pushed forward, believing that by keeping us together, I was doing the best for my son and our family. When the day finally came, just before our son turned five, we packed our bags, left behind our life in Bali, and set off for the Gold Coast with hopes for a brighter future and a chance to mend what felt irreparably broken.

Australia, for me, represented a fresh start — a chance to build something new for my family. As broken as our relationship was, I was determined to never give up, believing that a fresh start would help heal what seemed to be missing in previous years.

Within the second month of settling into a friend's home temporarily, I quickly found work as an electrical solar installer, securing some income to allow us to apply for a rental home. I threw myself into the grind, working tirelessly in the Australian heat while Lucy was in the midst of applying for permanent residency. But as much as I hoped that this new chapter would bring harmony to our relationship, it became evident that things were unraveling even further.

Despite my efforts to do right by Lucy, to provide, and to create stability, the cracks in our foundation deepened with what seemed like every corner being a wrong turn. I couldn't understand why things weren't improving, especially since I thought we had everything to be grateful for. I had a deep belief that this move would shift the dynamics between us, but instead, it highlighted the growing distance.

I had never pictured myself as part of a broken family. I had always dreamed of creating a happy, united household — a sanctuary for my child, unlike the fragmented upbringing I had experienced. I did all that I could to maintain this dream, but reality had other plans. The road we were on became increasingly rocky and I knew my son could see and hear everything.

This realization weighed on me like nothing else ever had. As a father, I was torn between my role as a provider and the overwhelming guilt of not being able to shield my son from the chaos that had crept into our home. The calmer I tried to be, the worse it got. No matter how much I tried, the emotional toll was immense and the strain on all of us became unbearable. My world crumbled when my marriage unfolded as though through flashbacks, scene by scene, with the realization of how blind I had been to the many red flags that had repeatedly occurred in front of me. Reflecting upon how I had not taken the necessary actions required throughout those years, I was struck with grief. However, it seemed that life had given me this path for some reason or another, so my only consolation through it all was a feeling that there was always a brighter side, and a deeper purpose for any pain I experienced.

Of all the hardships I had faced, this was the most difficult. It wasn't just the financial strain or the stress of rebuilding a life in a new country, it was the emotional battle of trying to hold together a family that was fracturing before my eyes. It challenged me in ways I had never experienced before, forcing me to confront fears, doubts, and insecurities that I hadn't even realized I carried.

Through it all, I kept going, not for myself, but for my son. He was my anchor, my reason to keep trying, even when everything felt like it was falling apart. And though the path ahead remained uncertain, I clung to the hope that brighter days were still possible — not just for me, but for the family I so desperately wanted to keep whole.

Stepping Away

When living together became too much to bear after a heated conversation one day, we both finally accepted that we could no longer be together. I was forced out of the rental home, which was in my name, and asked to take nothing but my clothes. So I packed a small bag and set out to buy a car — something cheap to sleep in for a few nights before I had to return to the job I had started only a few months earlier. I had nowhere else to go, and applying for another rental unit was not an option for at least some time because I was still covering the rent for the unit where my son and Lucy were living. Since the home was under my name, I couldn't apply for another rental because my weekly income was insufficient to pay for two rentals and ongoing costs. And so, the cycle began again. I found myself rationing every dollar, eating from cans, and scraping together just enough to keep covering Lucy's and our son's rent and food. It was all somewhat familiar to the experiences I'd had when I first arrived in the country.

Sometimes, no matter how much you fight against the current, the path forward requires the strength of letting go and moving with the current's flow.

I had come to accept that no one is perfect — not me, not Lucy, and not the circumstances that brought us together and tore us apart. But I couldn't help but ask myself, "How can I be greater than my past? How can I guide my son through this new reality, where he now lives in two different worlds, with two different perspectives?"

I realized then that my role as a father was not to shield him from life's challenges but to guide him through them. Like a captain navigating stormy seas, I had to be his anchor, his compass, and his steady hand, even when my own soul felt lost. The responsibility of being his guide was my purpose, my chance to show him strength even in the face of adversity.

The hardest part was reliving the reality I once knew, but this time, through my son. I saw in him the same confusion and questions I had carried as a child, torn and confused from living between two worlds — his mom's and his dad's — each of us with our differing values, perspectives, and emotions. My task became ensuring that he didn't feel the same isolation and loss of identity that I once felt.

It was easy to form the thought and its words, but infinitely harder to put it into practice. The more I gave of myself, the more challenges seemed to arise, as if the universe was testing my strength and using those challenges to teach me what I needed to learn. There were moments when I felt utterly drained, like a shell of my former self, questioning who I was and what my purpose had become. I truly felt lost and defeated by the constant knockdowns of life's challenges.

I found myself at a crossroads once again, restarting my life in two worlds: the life of a father navigating the complexities of co-parenting, and the life of a man rediscovering his own identity. It was a role I thought I had mastered, yet it felt new, raw, and overwhelming. This taught me that nothing can truly be mastered and that we are all continually learning.

But this time, I had a deeper understanding of what was at stake. It wasn't just about me anymore; it was about my son. The choices I made, the way I carried myself, and the love I showed him would hopefully instill good values. While the journey ahead seemed daunting, I knew I needed to hold his hand, walk beside him, and show him that I was there for him in the way I had hoped others would be there for me, but weren't; at least not quite as close as I intended to be for him. I had survived a challenge, just as the tides rose and fell, and now it was time to lift my head high and thrive — for myself and for my son. I hoped he would always look to me for guidance, no matter where he found himself in the unfolding chapters of his journey. I still do.

They say the early years shape a child — their emotions, beliefs, and behaviors all forming quietly between the ages of one and seven. He is now six and I remember my childhood like it was yesterday, so I know how true this statement is. Because our time together in this life is limited, I'll do my best with the time that remains on this ticking clock to always be loving and create memorable moments for us both.

CHAPTER VIII

The Endless Journey

As I bring this book to a close, I find myself pausing — not just to mark an ending, but to reflect on the journey itself. Life, I've come to realize, is a mosaic: a collection of moments, some fractured, some radiant, some seemingly ordinary. Yet each piece carries a blessing, even if it is hidden at first. Each experience, joyful or painful, contributes to the larger picture, teaching us, shaping us, and guiding us toward growth.

One theme runs through these pages like a steady current: resilience. Life's storms arrive unannounced. Plans falter, relationships strain, dreams are delayed. And yet, within each challenge lies a blessing — an opportunity to discover strength we didn't know we had, to learn lessons we might have otherwise missed, to grow into a more compassionate and capable version of ourselves. Resilience is not the absence of hardship; it is the ability to navigate it, to bend and recover, to see the blessing within the struggle and to emerge transformed.

Resilience, I've learned, is not about being unbreakable, it is about being adaptable. It is knowing when to stand firm, when to bend, and when to let go. And in that adaptability, there is blessing: the blessing of perspective, of patience, and of understanding that growth often comes not despite challenges, but because of them.

If life has taught me anything, it is this: we are shaped not by what happens to us, but by the choices we make in response. Without the highs and lows, there is no adventure, no opportunity to uncover the blessings hidden within each twist of fate. Every decision — whether cautious, impulsive, or daring — carries the power to shape our journey. I have stumbled, hesitated, and leapt into the unknown. Each choice, whether it brought success or failure, revealed a blessing — some obvious, some subtle, but each offering a lesson to carry forward.

We cannot always control life's currents, but we can choose how we navigate them. True power lies not in avoiding the waves, but in steering our ship with intention, courage, and gratitude, for even the storms bring blessings we may not yet see.

At its heart, this story is about connection: to family, friends, culture, and to ourselves. These connections anchor us, challenge us, and shape who we become. But connection is not always effortless; it asks for vulnerability, patience, and sometimes forgiveness. And yet, within every connection lies a blessing of love, understanding, and the quiet thread of shared humanity that shapes who we are. The strongest bonds are rarely built on perfection; they are forged in moments of empathy, compassion, and showing up, even when it seems difficult.

Life is, above all, a journey of self-discovery. It is about peeling back layers, facing our truths, and embracing the person we are becoming. My story — like yours — is unfinished. I have made mistakes, taken wrong turns, and doubted myself countless times. Yet each misstep revealed a hidden blessing, a new insight, or a strength I might never have known otherwise.

Self-discovery is not a destination; it is a process. It is about learning to love yourself while striving to grow. It is about honoring your past without being imprisoned by it. And it is about uncovering the blessings along the way, understanding that every step — no matter how small — carries meaning and offers opportunity.

As you finish reading the last few chapters of this book, take a moment to reflect: Which chapters have defined you? Which lessons have shaped your path? And most importantly, which blessings have revealed themselves, sometimes quietly, sometimes in plain sight, guiding you to this very moment?

Life is not a straight road. It winds, twists, and surprises. There will be victories and losses, joys and sorrows. And yet, through it all, there is growth, there is learning, and there is the endless possibility of uncovering the blessings hidden in every experience.

Between The Lines: When Life Writes Its Own Story

Watching my son navigate childhood, I'm struck by how life often comes full circle. The boy who once feared sleeping alone, struggled to find his place between worlds, and questioned where he truly belonged now understands that these challenges have shaped his greatest strengths.

My journey — from a child who lost his mother at two, to being raised by a Balinese family while looking nothing like them, to navigating multiple schools and cultures — might seem like a story of loss and displacement. But now, I see it differently. Each apparent setback was a gift wrapped in beautiful, unexpected packaging.

The loss of my birth mother brought me Berate, whose love taught me that family transcends blood. My father's unconventional path showed me that life's greatest adventures often begin with a step away from the expected. The challenge of moving between languages and cultures has given me the ability to see the world through multiple lenses, understanding that truth often lies in the spaces between perspectives.

Perhaps the most profound lesson emerged from what once seemed like my greatest struggles — the feeling of never quite fitting in. What I initially saw as a burden, I now recognize as a blessing. Being between worlds has taught me that we don't have to choose one way of being. We can be many things at once: Western and Eastern, traditional and modern, rooted and free.

Sometimes, what seems to be our deepest wounds become our greatest gifts. What feels like displacement might be life positioning us for a broader perspective. The ability to navigate between worlds is a strength, not a weakness. Family isn't about matching appearances but about hearts that choose to beat together. Every ending carries within it the seed of a new beginning, a quiet blessing in disguise.

CHAPTER IX

Musings, Philosophy, and Practical Insights

Spirituality

Morning prayers in our household were a way to honor and respect the unseen, fostering a balance between the visible and the invisible realms. This practice was, at its heart, an acknowledgment that our very existence on this island, or any land, is a granted permission — that we are but guests here. To live well, we must adhere to the land's rules, respecting the spirit and physical nature of the place where we reside.

We lived by the universal principle of "what you put out, you get back," which is the heart of this necessary balance. This balance, however, is not a static state of rest, but a constant, magnetic dance — an adventure of opposing forces that want to pull you entirely to one side or the other. Life is the vibrant energy of navigating this perpetual tension. It was a practice embedded deeply in our Balinese traditions.

However, this ritual ceased when I moved in with my sister. It was not until I experienced disturbances in my own bed in Made and Mark's house that I fully grasped the importance of maintaining this balance and honoring the unseen permissions. Unbeknownst to me as a child placing prayer offerings, I had been practicing a powerful lesson in living in respectful reciprocity with the world.

Inspiring Beyond the Horizon

My lifelong aspiration was to be a leader; not just any leader, but one who inspires action and ignites change. Early on, I believed that to lead, I first had to follow. Yet, as I journeyed through life's various challenges and roles, I discovered that true leadership isn't about following someone else's path; it's about forging your own path through the inspiration of others.

A true leader ignites a fire in others, motivating them to lead in their own right. This type of leadership creates a cycle of inspiration, where each individual is both a leader and a learner, continuously driven by passion rather than obligation.

Consider the conventional view of politicians as leaders. Often, they seem to lead not for the communal benefit but to perpetuate their own status, trapped in cycles of short-term gains and superficial achievements. They maintain a façade of leadership without fostering genuine trust or investment in the collective good. This misalignment between their actions and the true needs of the people only perpetu-

ates disillusionment and passivity among the popu-
lace.

Awareness: The Compass of My Journey

One of the fundamental tools that significantly shaped my journey is the practice of awareness. This concept encompasses virtually every aspect of life. I was introduced to it early on through the wisdom of Balinese culture. Awareness acts as a pivot that balances our thoughts and actions. Mark, who often guided me in my younger years, emphasized the importance of thinking before speaking; of carefully considering ideas and responses before expressing them.

By practicing this, I gained a deeper understanding of others' perspectives, reducing assumptions and misinterpretations.

The application of awareness is both versatile and profound. Mastering this skill has been instrumental in navigating the highs and lows of my life, providing a steady hand through its many challenges and changes.

Success Redefined

What is success? Throughout my young years in Bali, it was common to hear people wishing each other success during their interactions with phrases like "I wish you all the success" or "Hopefully you have success" echoing through daily conversations. Initially, I associated success with wealth, believing that a plentiful amount of money equated to a successful life.

However, the birth of my child shifted my perspective dramatically. I realized that success isn't about financial accumulation; rather, it's about fulfilling your potential. Success isn't measured by how you stack up against others but by comparing what you have achieved to what you could have achieved. It's a personal benchmark, not a universal standard.

For years, I was misled by a common misunderstanding of success, always seeking more and believing that the next job position and paycheck would bring fulfillment. This endless ladder seemed to grow taller with every rung I climbed. But true success isn't about money or continual accumulation; it's uniquely personal and defined by our own values and goals.

I once obsessed over being successful in everything — a mindset that led me down many rabbit holes. Success is about achieving what matters most to us, not what is expected by society or dictated by external pressures.

In the journey of my life, each thread of failure has been woven into a broader tapestry of resilience and understanding. From the serene shores of Bali to the bustling streets of Sydney, my journey has been marked not just by moments of triumph but also by instances of profound setbacks. Each stumble and fall taught me a critical lesson — that failure is not the antithesis of success but, often, its precursor.

Reflecting on the times I felt lost, when each decision seemed to lead to another dead end, I now see these not as defeats but as vital moments of learning. For instance, the early days at my sister's factory, where I was thrust into a role that I was utterly unprepared for, initially felt like a series of unending challenges. My inexperience was glaring and the skepticism from seasoned workers was palpable. Yet, it was there, in the heart of discomfort and uncertainty, that I found profound strength and unexpected mentorship in the wisdom of the local artisans.

The practice of stepping back to assess each failure, understanding its roots, and adapting my approach has been instrumental. This mindful contemplation and reflecting on what went wrong, why it happened, and how to adjust transformed potential defeats into lessons that propelled me forward. It was a shift in perspective, a realization that success is not a clear, unobstructed path but a winding road filled with obstacles meant to refine our ambitions and clarify our desires.

The Balinese philosophy of *Tri Hita Karana*, emphasizing harmony with people, nature, and the spiritual, further reinforced this understanding. It taught me that balance in life's pursuits, including how we handle failure, is crucial. Success, therefore, isn't about avoiding failure but about embracing it as an inevitable, enriching part of the journey.

The Art of Living in Multiple Worlds

Some of us are born into one world and remain within its familiar rhythms for a lifetime. Others, whether by chance, choice, or necessity, find themselves stretched between multiple worlds, carrying pieces of each, never fully belonging to just one. This is both a privilege and a paradox.

To live between worlds is to exist in a space of constant transition. It is to know the customs of one place while learning the language of another, to feel at home in multiple spaces yet somehow never entirely rooted in any. It is to carry the weight of tradition in one hand and the pull of change in the other, forever balancing the tension between the two.

At times, this existence feels like a gift. It grants us the ability to move fluidly, to adapt and to understand perspectives that others may never encounter. We become bridges — between cultures, between people, between ways of thinking. We see the world through multiple lenses and in doing so, we cultivate a deeper sense of empathy and a broader understanding of what it means to be human.

But there is a quiet challenge in this too. To be between worlds is also to feel a certain kind of displacement — a lingering question of where, exactly, we belong. One world calls us back with the comfort of familiarity, while another urges us forward with the thrill of possibility. In moments of solitude, we wonder: Are we destined to always be in motion, never fully arriving?

And yet, perhaps this is the secret — we are not meant to arrive. We are meant to evolve. The space between worlds is not an exile, but an invitation, an opportunity to weave together the best of each, to build something new out of all we have absorbed. Identity is not a destination; it is a conversation, a constant becoming.

We are shaped by where we come from, but we are not confined by it. The traditions we inherit do not have to be walls; they can be doorways. The new worlds we step into do not have to erase the old; they can expand them. And the tension we feel is not a burden but a sign of growth — proof that we are no longer who we once were, but not yet who we are becoming.

If there is a lesson in living between worlds, it is this: we do not have to choose. We do not have to decide between past and future, between belonging and seeking, between what we were given and what we create. We are allowed to be both — to honor where we've been while embracing where we are going.

And so, the question is not where we belong, but rather: How can we carry each world with us? How can we let them shape us without confining us? How can we live in the in-between with grace?

Perhaps the answer lies in surrendering to the movement itself. In recognizing that every place we have touched, every culture we have absorbed, and every relationship that has shaped us — these do not make us divided. They make us whole.

The Cycle of Life: Where There's a Fall, There's a Replacement

I once stood beneath a tree in autumn, watching its leaves fall one by one. Each one seemed to hesitate, as if reluctant to let go of the branch that had held it for so long. And yet, as they drifted to the ground, I couldn't help but notice how the earth welcomed them not as an end, but as a beginning. The fallen leaves would nourish the soil, preparing the way for new growth when spring arrived.

Life, I've come to realize, moves in much the same way. It's a cycle of endings and beginnings, of falling and rising, of loss and renewal. When something slips away — a relationship, a dream, a sense of stability — it can feel like the ground beneath us is crumbling. But what if, like those leaves, we're not falling into emptiness but into possibility? What if every ending is simply making space for something new to take root?

I've often wondered why it's so hard to see this in the moment. When we're in the midst of loss, it's easy to feel stuck, as if the world has left us behind. But time has a way of revealing what we can't yet see. That job in the photography studio I thought I'd lost forever? It led me to a path I never would have chosen otherwise. The heartbreak that felt like it would never heal? It taught me how to love more deeply, both myself and others.

The past, with all its twists and turns, is like the soil beneath our feet. It's the foundation of who we are, rich with the lessons of what we've lived through. Even the hardest moments — the falls, the failures, the disappointments — have a way of shaping us, of preparing us for what's to come. And just as a tree doesn't mourn its fallen leaves, we too can learn to trust in the cycles of life.

But here's the paradox: while the past shapes us, it's the present that carries us forward. The future is always on the horizon, a promise of new seasons, new growth. But we can't reach it by clinging to what's already gone. We have to be here, now, fully present in this moment. It's the only place where life truly happens and the only place where we can plant the seeds of what's to come.

So, I ask myself: What am I holding onto that no longer serves me? What am I afraid to let go of, even though it's already slipping away? And what might be waiting to take its place, if only I could trust the cycle enough to release my grip?

Life, like the seasons, doesn't ask for our permission to change. It simply moves, carrying us along with it. And maybe that's the beauty of it all: the falling, the letting go, the rising again. Maybe it's not about controlling the cycle but learning to dance with it, to trust that every ending is just the beginning of something new.

Appendix:
Bali's History

The Eternal Guardian of Bali

Bali is more than just a name; it is a story. Early stone inscriptions combine Sanskrit with Old Javanese to give rise to the name "Walidwipa," meaning "Sacred Island" or "Island of Offerings," a place of worship where rituals and devotion unite its inhabitants with the unseen. Yet, beyond these inscriptions, Bali embodies a deeper significance as a balance between worlds, where gods and mortals coexist and every offering restores harmony between the visible and the invisible.

Stepping onto Bali is like entering something timeless, where past and present converge, where spirits reside and stories breathe. With relatively little written history, memory is shaped through myths, rituals, and the voices of ancestors. Much of what we know is influenced by those who came before us, allowing for both wonder and interpretation in the story that follows.

The Voice of the Island

Before men walked these shores, before temples rose to the heavens, and before the dance of fire and shadow cast its eternal rhythm, there was me.

I am Dewa Bayu, the wind whispering through what they call my sacred banyan tree. I have no beginning nor end. I am the pulse of waves against white sands and the ember of fire nearby. I am the spirit of Bali; its memory. I have watched as the first feet pressed into my soil, the ancients carved their destinies into the stones, and the gods weaved their magic in the air.

I have seen kingdoms rise and fall, their rulers leaving nothing but whispers on the wind. I have heard the cries of warriors, the prayers of priests, and the laughter of children running through rice fields. I have danced in the firelight with shamans and I have shed tears through wars. I am the keeper of stories. And I will tell you these stories now, not as history written in stone, but as it truly was — alive, breathing, filled with triumph, sorrow, and the essence of the island it has now become.

The First People (3000 BCE - 9th Century)

The land was wild and the animals thrived long before Bali had a name, before the existence of temples, palaces, or kings. Volcanoes rumbled, dense jungles covered the island, and rivers carved paths through the valleys. The sea whispered to the shore from the Austronesian lands, and for thousands of years, I was alone, digging into the soil each year and watching over this land. But one day, they came.

They arrived in small wooden canoes, their bronzed skin glistening and wide eyes filled with wonder, having crossed the sea by following the stars and the call of the wind. "Who are you?" I whispered through the trees. The shamans, those attuned to the unseen, heard me. They pressed their hands into the earth and left small offerings of fruit and flowers. They carved symbols in stone to appease the gods watching over this new land. I smiled and blessed their steps.

Those first people built their homes near the rivers in what would become Cekik. Handmade stone tools and baskets and hunting became their specialties. They learned the rhythms of the land, the language of animals, and the soul of the mountains.

For a time, they lived together in peace, but they were not alone. Others lurked in the jungle, hidden in the mist. These were leyaks, the dark creatures that the people feared. The balance was maintained by the Barong, the ancient protectors, and by Rangda, the weaver of chaos, who was always watching, always waiting. One night, the first fire along the shore ignited when a storm arose not from the sky, but from the atmosphere. Rangda's voice slithered through the wind: "Bali is mine."

Standing among the people, I replied with a firm, "No, it is theirs now." Thus, the first battle of light versus dark was not fought with swords, but with dreams that compelled people to confront their own souls.

The First Kings & the Coming of the Gods (8th - 10th Century)

Time passed and the first villages evolved into towns. The people constructed simple shrines of wood and stone, bridges connecting their world to the spirit realm. They danced under the moonlight, shared tales by the fire, and gave daily offerings.

Then something new arrived from the west. Bali was visited by priests from the great Hindu kingdoms of Java, who brought holy texts and gold idols to the island. They spoke of magnificent temples and powerful kings alongside their mighty gods: Shiva, Brahma, and Vishnu. However, the Balinese did not flee their old gods. They did not reject their spirits; instead, they embraced the new, mixing ancient traditions into something wholly unique and syncretic.

It was during this era that Bali's first true ruler, Sri Kesari Warmadewa, emerged from Java. His message was a promise carried through time: "I am Sri Kesari, chosen by the gods. I have come to bring order and to make Bali a home for the divine."

Under his rule, temples rose like mountains from the earth. Great stone shrines were built by the people to connect the visible and unseen realms. The temples were not merely places of worship; they were bridges between humans and spirits, between gods, and between the past and the future.

Yet behind every light, there is shadow. The leyaks, who once hid in the darkness, gained new followers. Some rulers heeded their whispers, yearning for influence beyond the physical realm. Shadows spread across the land, and for the first time, Bali trembled with uncertainty.

I whispered to the wind, "What will happen to this island?"

The answer came not from the spirits, but from the east. The eyes of a great empire were turning toward Bali; the Majapahit were coming.

The Rise of the Majapahit (13th - 14th Century)

For centuries, Bali existed as its own world — a place of spirits, gods, kings, temples, and warriors, embodying the struggle of light versus shadow; yet change was imminent.

The Majapahit Empire rose from the east, ruling over all the islands of the archipelago. They were warriors, traders, and builders of great cities. They had now set their sights on Bali.

I, Dewa Bayu, had witnessed empires come and go, but this one was different. This one emerged from

Gajah Mada, Majapahit's greatest prime minister. He was more than a man — he was a storm that changed history.

"I will unite the islands," Gajah Mada declared in his Palapa Oath. "I will not stop until all the archipelago is under one rule." That vision included Bali.

As the first ships arrived on the shores of Bali in the late 13th century, they came not as friends but as conquerors. The Majapahit army was a completely new experience for the Balinese, compromising thousands of armoured warriors carrying traditional weapons produced in Java's great foundries. They advanced through the valleys with banners raised and chants echoing.

The Balinese resisted with all their strength: warriors wielding spears and swords, priests invoking good spirits, and shamans casting protective spells. The Barong was called upon by its people to combat the dark forces threatening to consume Bali.

Gajah Mada was relentless in his mission, employing strategy to turn Balinese kings against one another, offering them power in exchange for loyalty. One by one, the great kingdoms of Bali fell.

By the early 14th century, the Majapahit had taken control. Bali was no longer just an island; it had become part of an empire. The Majapahit brought with them a wave of Javanese culture, introducing new religions, crafts, and customs. Temples expanded in size, their gates pointing skyward. Javanese architects meticulously constructed the pura — sacred temple complexes whose carvings told tales of gods and demons.

The inhabitants of Bali did not lose their individuality; instead, they transformed. The island embraced the very best of what the Majapahit offered and made it their own. The dances grew richer, the stories more complex, and the connection with the divine deepened. This period saw the birth of the unique Balinese Hinduism that exists today. However, not everything was well. The spirits of the land became restless as the Majapahit rulers took over and the balance began to shift. The transfer of power from priests to kings was in progress. The whispers of ancestors and ancient traditions were becoming lost in the clamor of politics and war. Just as the Majapahit seemed unstoppable, the empire itself began to collapse.

The Fall of the Majapahit and The Return of Bali's Soul (15th - 16th Century)

It had been a gradual collapse. First, the trade routes disintegrated, followed by power struggles. The Majapahit kings turned against one another and their empire weakened with each battle.

The spread of Islam from the west emerged as a new force in Java, leading to the fall of the great Hindu kingdoms. Majapahit, once the largest empire in the region, struggled to survive. In the early 16th century, the Majapahit nobles, priests, and artists departed Java and crossed the sea in search of a place where their gods would still be revered and their customs would endure.

They arrived in Bali, the last stronghold of the Majapahit spirit. Now isolated from Java, the rulers declared their independence. The Balinese kings, once subjects of the empire, now ruled in their own right.

They brought new art, traditions and knowledge with them. The grand culture of Majapahit found its final home in Bali, merging once again with the island's traditional culture. However, fear accompanied their arrival. They were aware of what had transpired in Java and understood how quickly empires could crumble. As a result, they built fortifications, strengthened their armies, and prepared for the day when a new threat would emerge. That day was not far away.

The Kingdoms of Bali (16th - 19th Century)

Bali had been left alone after the collapse of the Majapahit Empire. It transformed into a kingdom of kings, no longer a colony of Java, with each king vying for dominance and claiming to be the true leader of the island. For centuries, Bali was not a single kingdom but a collection of many.

Klungkung was the home of the Dewa Agung, the supreme ruler of the island. Buleleng, independent and fierce, guarded the northern coast.

Karangasem was a group of warriors and traders whose influence extended beyond Bali. Mengwi, Badung, Gianyar, and Tabanan each had their own kings, armies, and ambitions. They were sometimes allies but more often rivals.

The Balinese kingdoms were adorned with temples, golden palaces, and vast rice fields. Dance, music, and storytelling evolved into refined art forms. Wayang Kulit, a type of shadow puppetry, conveyed stories to the people. Legong and kecak dancing became popular pastimes performed in temple courtyards at night. But beneath the beauty, war was constant.

The kings made efforts to expand their territories, and their armies marched against one another. The construction of fortresses, the burning of villages, and the formation and dissolution of alliances were all part of the struggle. The balance of power was always shifting.

While the kings battled, the gods sat and watched. I whispered to the wind, "This isn't the way; Bali is not meant for endless war." The kings did not hear me.

The kingdoms of Bali governed themselves for generations, unaffected by outside forces. They had witnessed the Dutch arrive in Java, stealing land and destroying empires. Yet, Bali remained free. But that freedom would not last. A storm was approaching. The Balinese had never encountered a force like this before. The Dutch were watching. Soon, they would arrive.

The Fall of the Kingdoms (19th - Early 20th Century)

The kings of Bali had ruled for hundreds of years, their temples reaching for the sky and their warriors fighting off invaders. Whispers in the wind spoke of a greater foe than ever before. I, Dewa Bayu, had seen the Dutch sailing large ships, promising kings trade, alliances, and gold. This time was different. They were not here to converse; they were here to take.

A Gathering Storm (1846 - 1906)

When the Dutch arrived in the north, they brought cannons and muskets to Buleleng and sent a force unlike any the Balinese had seen before. The warriors fought with kris blades in the sun, but the Dutch had firepower that could pierce stone. All the fortresses fell at once, marking the fall of a huge northern kingdom. Its people had spirits that would not bow as easily as the southern kings; Badung, Klungkung, Karangasem, and Tabanan refused to yield. They sharpened their blades, raised their priests, and called upon the gods. Bali needed to be taken by force if the Dutch wanted it, and so the battle began.

The streets of Denpasar were quiet as the Dutch marched in. Balinese warriors did not hide or beg for mercy. Instead, they wore white, marched forward, and met death with open arms. This was called the Puputan: fighting until death, without surrender.

The king of Badung led the way with his kris in hand and a calm expression. Behind him, his warriors and even priests joined him. They knew they could not win, but victory was never the goal. "Better to die free than live under a foreign king," the king declared.

The Dutch opened fire, yet the Balinese pressed forward, never surrendering. The soil became bloody, but they continued to advance. Their spirits carried them into the unseen world that surrounds those who remained.

Two years later, Klungkung fell in a similar manner. The last Balinese king viewed his people from the palace steps. "We return to the gods," he said, before stepping into the blazing fire.

Bali was conquered but not broken. The Dutch took the land and its people for farming and the spice trade, but they could not claim the soul of the people or their island. The temples remained, and still, people prayed. The Barong danced under the moonlight and the spirits continued to speak. I, Dewa Bayu, watched, waiting. This was not the end; there was more to come. And this time, it would shake the world.

The War That Changed Everything (1942 - 1945)

Years passed in quiet Bali. The Dutch took the island, but not its spirit. Temples stood, prayers continued, and souls of warriors roamed the land.

Then came new ships; this time not from the Dutch but from Japan. The Dutch were strong, but the Japanese were relentless. They stormed Bali's shores, spreading their empire across the islands. The Dutch fled and their rule collapsed overnight. For the first time, Bali was free of foreign kings. But this freedom was not to last. The Japanese imposed a different kind of rule — hard, merciless, unyielding. They made the Balinese work, fight, and serve their empire. The people bowed, but their hearts remained strong.

I, Dewa Bayu, spoke through the wind and whispered to my people, "Hold on; the storm is almost over."

The Last Battle (1945)

Then, the gods sent a new sign from the skies — fire rained down. The world shook as World War II reached its violent peak. Japan faltered and their empire began to crack. Sensing weakness, the Balinese rose once more. The warrior spirit that had once fought the Dutch now fought the Japanese, refusing to live as slaves in their own land. The war ended in flames and Japan surrendered. For the first time in hundreds of years, Indonesia declared independence on August 17, 1945, and Bali finally had a chance to become its own.

The Final Fight for Freedom (1945 - 1949)

But the Dutch were not done. As soon as the Japanese left, they tried to return. They thought Bali, like the rest of Indonesia, would bow once more, but they were wrong.

A warrior who had witnessed the unfolding of his own land through the years rose; his name was I Gusti Ngurah Rai. Bali's warriors gathered for one final stand at Margarana in 1946. Outnumbered and outgunned, they fought with fire in their hearts. "There will be no surrender," the colonel declared. Ngurah Rai and his men fell and their sacrifice burned like a torch through the land. The world was watching now. The Dutch could not keep what was no longer theirs. In 1949, after years of resistance, the Dutch finally left Bali in peace. Bali was finally free.

The kings were gone and its warriors had fallen. But Bali's spirit remained in the mountains, the rivers, the temples, and in each prayer.

"Bali belongs to no empire," I, Dewa Bayu, whispered in the wind. "It belongs to its people and always will."

And so, the island stood not as a conquered land, but as a place where the beautiful spirits of its people remained, where warriors never truly died, and where the past still breathed in every temple stone, reminding us that balance and harmony are the way.

Bali was not lost.

Bali is eternal.

About the Author

Luca De Coney is an introspective writer whose work explores the quiet truths that shape the human experience. Through his reflective storytelling, he invites readers to uncover the beauty hidden within life's trials and transformations.

Bali's Son: Uncovering life's hidden Blessings is more than a memoir; it's a mirror for anyone who has ever questioned why life happens the way it does. Luca writes not to teach, but to remind us that within every wound lies wisdom, and within every ending, the beginning of something divine.

If this story resonated with you, I'd love to hear from you.

You can find and contact me on:

@deconey

@deconey

lucadeconeymjt@gmail.com

www.ingramcontent.com/pod-product-compliance
Lightning Source LLC
Chambersburg PA
CBHW021242060726
47590CB00005B/1861